M000219342

What reviewers, writers, and editors say about *Reed's Homophones:*

*R*eed's Homophones is the handiest quick reference on the subject. Writers, editors, students, teachers, business and government folks—I can't imagine anyone anywhere in the world who would not welcome this chance to make the world of words a friendlier place. Even prophets may profit. Mastery would not take long, but stopping once you start—as with whipped cream or kissing—may take more willpower than most folks have.

David Madden, Pulitzer-Prize nominee for *The Suicide's Wife*,
author of *Abducted by Circumstance* and many other books

*R*eed's Homophones: *A Comprehensive Book of Sound-alike Words* should be in any collection strong in English language explorations, literature, and wordsmithing, whether for school-age readers in high school to college, or general-interest collections appealing to writers and authors... While reading a dictionary might not be everyone's cup of tea, *Reed's Homophones* serves as both an at-a-glance desk reference for writers and as a word nerd's browsing delight... Reference collections strong in writer's guides should consider *Reed's Homophones* a key acquisition.

Diane Donovan, Donovan's Bookshelf
Midwest Book Review

*T*his slim gem of a book belongs on every reference shelf, whether for use by the professional writer or those who write simply for pleasure—an invaluable addition for those who love accuracy and polish in their writing. Written with a deft touch and flourishes of humor, *Reed's Homophones* should not be missed.

Sharon Shervington, former editor, international division, *The Wall Street Journal*

Whether one calls these mistakes malapropisms or mondegreens, a misspelling or a mispronunciation, *Reed's Homophones* is a perfect resource for students to have alongside their *Roget's Thesaurus* and their *Webster's Dictionary*.

Dr. Arnold D. Sgan, retired education consultant

This is a reference book, and a very helpful one at that. It is not designed as a page-turner. But I found it so interesting, I actually read it from one end to the other ... That's how interesting and entertaining it turned out to be. It is also very educational as a tool for building your own vocabulary. A must for every writer, for sure, and for everyone interested in the English language.

Fred Flaxman, author of award-winning memoir *Sixty Slices of Life ... on Wry*

Move over, Webster, Oxford, Partridge, and Roget, and make room on the bookshelf for Reed. I prophesy that *Reed's Homophones* will be as well-thumbed as any of them.

If only *Reed's Homophones* had been around when I was riding herd [heard] on newspaper reporters; just think of how many blue [blew] pencils I could have saved, how much aggravation we would have been spared. So thank you, A.D. Reed ... better late than never!

Glennys Christie, former newspaper editor and publisher

I've done editing since the 1960s, and this book is an essential tool for combatting Spell Check. For anyone who believes that "Spill Czech cant bee beet four-hour porpoises," *Reed's Homophones* is an absolute blessing.

Marshall Lancaster, copy editor

Reed's reference book should be front and center on every writer's shelf. His work has made the English language much easier to navigate.

F. "Ted" Alexander, author, *The Fall of Summer* and *After and Before*

REED'S HOMOPHONES
A COMPREHENSIVE BOOK OF
SOUND-ALIKE WORDS

(including some borrowed from other tongues, and a few that
aren't quite homophonic, but are awfully close)

As well as frequent

misspellings,
mispronunciations,
misused word pairs,
schizophrenic antonyms,

and a few pet peeves

Fourth Edition
Revised & Expanded

A. D. Reed

Pisgah Press was established in 2011 to publish and promote works of quality offering original ideas and insight into the human condition, the realm of knowledge, and the world around us.

Copyright © 2012, 2018 Pisgah Press

Printed in the United States of America

Published by Pisgah Press, LLC
PO Box 9663, Asheville, NC 28815
www.pisgahpress.com

Cover design by MyOwnEditor.com

All rights reserved. No part of this publication may be reproduced, stored in a retrieval system, or transmitted, in any form or by any means, electronic, mechanical, photocopying, recording, or otherwise, without the prior written permission of Pisgah Press, except in the case of quotations in critical articles or reviews.

Library of Congress Cataloging-in-Publication Data
Reed, A. D.
Reed's Homophones (Revised): A comprehensive book of sound-alike words /A. D. Reed

ISBN: 978-1942016427
Language Arts & Disciplines/Reference

Fourth Edition
June 2018
Third Printing
June 2020
Fourth Printing
June 2022

A note about the

Origins

of this book and my

Acknowledgments

of those who helped make it possible,
along with words of

Thanks

to all and sundry

The mother of this book was a series of mistakes in word use that cropped up in my local newspaper over a period of months beginning in 2007. Its father was a useful but irritating habit, inherited from my parents, of correcting errors wherever and however they arise. Those two factors engendered a short list of common homophones that seem to attract newspaper reporters as honey does flies. Houses are "raised" by fires; actors demonstrate real "flare" on stage; people wait with "baited" breath; the view through the picture window is a "site" to behold; witnesses are rarely "fazed" but often "phased." Et cetera.

So first let me express deep gratitude for my original inspiration to those Gannett journalists who write well, but not always right, and to their editors, whose oversight makes for good copy, but whose oversights allow the bad to sneak in as well. Second, of course, I thank my late father and mother, Mr. Nit and Mrs. Pick.

When my list of homophones had grown to several hundred, I shared it with lifelong friend, superb proofreader, and talented copy editor Carol Emmet. In addition to catching errors, she often responded with additional word pairs of her own, and over time helped more than anyone else in shaping this book.

My sister, the editor Claudette Upton, also gave me invaluable feedback before her untimely death, as did writers and editors Nelda Holder, Mary McClurkin, and Sarah-Ann Smith.

Once the book reached critical mass, I shared the text with my good friends Annick and the late Fred Flaxman, she a French-born, bilingual proofreader and he a retired radio and television writer and producer (and author of the hilarious memoir, *Sixty Slices of Life ... on Wry*; and with passionate readers Fiona Dudley and the late Greta Patterson. They all caught more mistakes and omissions in the manuscript and raised valuable questions that improved the book.

Since the book first appeared, readers have sent me numerous additional word pairs that appear in this most recent edition. In particular I'm grateful to former teacher Jane Vangemeren for her handwritten additions, and to Lou Gottlieb for his extensive lists, compiled over a lifetime of love of wordplay, and his eagle-eyed proofreading. Thanks to such correspondents, the book now contains well over 1,000 entries.

My profound thanks to all those above-named friends and colleagues for their kindness and generosity in reviewing this book before strangers could enjoy the opportunity to find the last overlooked error (it's in there somewhere—striving for perfection doesn't mean one ever reaches it).

And in advance I thank you, the reader, as well: I've inserted blank space after some sections so you can write in your own additions, discoveries, pet peeves, or other thoughts, and share them with me. This is a book that begs to be scribbled in ... so please do.

A. D. Reed

invade

inveighed

penitence

penitents

Contents

REED'S HOMOPHONES

Turn the page and
take a *peek*:
my *pique*
is at its *peak*.

What Are Homophones?

Homophones (also called homonyms, though they're not quite the same) are words that sound alike but have different meanings and, usually, spellings. Some are near misses, like "desperate" and "disparate": the first of the two begins with a rhyme for "desk", the second with "disk." But because most of us don't enunciate as clearly as we should, and regional accents can cause words that shouldn't sound similar to do so, I've included quite a few of them.

On the other hand, some words aren't quite close enough to be listed as homophones, but do make it into the list of "Easily misused, confused, and mistyped words"—such as "disillusion" and "dissolution."

And some disagreements will continue, like the lengthy discussion I had with my good friend Mary about the pronunciation of "axis." She preferred to append the "k" to the "a-" and the "s" to the "-is," leading to the pronunciation "ak-sis" shown in dictionaries. I consider the "x" a diphthong, pronounced "ks," leading to the pronunciation "a-ksis."

My approach is to imagine being interrupted in the middle of the word so as to discover where I stop making the sound. If you start to enunciate the spoken sounds of the phrase "the X axis" and interrupt yourself at various points, you'll break the syllables' component parts this way: "the" "e-" "ks" "a-" "ks-" "is." I don't believe anyone would break at "ek-" or "ak-" In fact, as we know from singing, our speech system depends on vowels, not consonants, to carry a tune. On the open end of a musical phrase—whether a full measure or a hemidemisemiquaver—we keep voicing the vowel while waiting for the next note, and we use a consonant—whether the hard "k" or the diphthong "ks"—to show us the end of one note or phrase and start the next.

Such disputes about the spoken language are one thing; those *writing* in English should bear in mind that some computer spell-checking systems can't determine which of several words you mean, only whether or not it's spelled correctly. As a result, if you write "fair" when you mean "fare," your spell check

3

software might not protect you from the busybody who writes or emails to complain about the misused word in your ad, website, blog, tweet, newspaper column, or wherever it showed up. (As a lifelong busybody myself, I know the syndrome only too well.)

In this collection, each set of homophones is listed alphabetically; in a few cases the second or third word is also listed, in a sort of reverse dictionary (for example, both "right" and "write" appear with their other shared homophones "rite" and "wright"). I've also included a few familiar French and Spanish words that we English speakers use but habitually confuse, misuse, or abuse.

Some words show up in several lists, being extraordinarily prone to confusion. Finally, from time to time a word is almost—though not quite—a homophone with another, but can be heard as such, especially for those for whom English is not the native tongue. In those cases the "almost-homophone" appears in parentheses, as on p. 56, "muscle" and "mussel" + "(muzzle)."

Many words listed have only one part of speech, which is usually apparent. When a word has more than one part of speech, each is identified by a

---

Does it really matter how I spell a simple, one-syllable word?

au   as in   Prime rib **au** jus

aux   " "   La Cage **aux** Folles

eau   " "   **Eau** Clair, Wisconsin

O!   " "   **O**, say can you see?

oh   " "   Uh-**oh**!

owe   " "   You **owe** it to yourself.

Oh! I guess maybe it does.

parenthetical "adj." (adjective), "adv." (adverb), "conj." (conjunction), "contr." (contraction), "exclam." (exclamation), "interj." (interjection), "n." (noun), "prep." (preposition), "pron." (pronoun), or "v." (verb). Origins are indicated when needed by "Fr." (French), "It." (Italian), "Sp." (Spanish), "Br." (British), "Ger." (German), "Lat." (Latin), "bibl." (biblical), etc.; usages by "arch." (archaic), "colloq." (colloquial), "dim." (diminutive), "fig." (figurative), "obs." (obsolete), and "sl." (slang). I also use "p." for "past" in "past participle" and "past tense."

Unlike dictionaries, this book does not have separate entries for each derivative of a word. "Tic" and "tick" are paired, but not their plurals; following "cell" (zygote; monk's room; prison enclosure) and "sell" (exchange for money; retail; convince), you will not find "cells" and "sells"; however, "cellar" and "seller," which form a separate pair of homophones, are listed. With a few exceptions, only when a plural or past tense is matched with a different homophone does it appear: for example, "ad" and "add" are listed as homophones, and, since "ads" is a homophone for "adze" as well as "adds," it appears as a separate entry.

I created this book primarily for two groups. First, it's aimed at writers and editors—not just professionals, but business owners and marketing executives and website owners and bloggers and ... —and anyone who wants to write well enough that the words they use don't come back to haunt or embarrass them. Pronunciation that is similar, though not truly homophonic, is often enough to trip them up; hence, many not-quite-homophones are included. Second, it's for students of the English language: I hope it will prove valuable to those in high school and college, to adults working on advanced degrees, and to anyone learning or teaching English as a Second Language (or even hoping to improve their Scrabble® game).

It's not a complete list; long after I began compiling it I still occasionally hear a spoken word, misinterpret it, and realize that I've stumbled across another homophone (or encountered, or even created, a mondegreen [see p. 133]). Since the first printing in 2011, I've come across scores more pairs that are included in this fourth edition. Some are as obvious as "cousin" and "cozen," originally (and unaccountably) overlooked; others are less common, like "boatswain," "boson," and "bosun"; and a few are as roll-your-eyes-inducing as "weal," "we'll," and "wheel." When others pop into your head the way they do into mine, don't hesitate to contact me (pisgahpress@gmail.com) so I can add them, too.

A. D. Reed

Note to self: Add these.

annunciation   enunciation

bollix   bollocks

heroin   heroine

pekoe   picot

subtler   sutler

triptik   triptych

Homophones A to Z

A

a – one, an

aahed – (v.) cried in delight, surprise

access – a way in

acclamation – praise

ad – advertisement, commercial

adds, ads – pl. of add, ad

ade – fruit drink, nectar

ae – one (Scot.)

odd – strange, peculiar; not divisible by two (arithmetic)

axis – line on a grid

acclimation – getting accustomed to

add – join, unite, increase

adz or **adze** – a cutting tool; axe

aid – (v.) help, assist; (n.) emergency assistance (*first a.*)

aide – assistant; subordinate (*a.-de-camp*)

adherence – faithfulness; abiding by rules, covenants, etc.; adhesion, as w. glue

adherents – followers; group members

adolescence – period of human development between childhood and adulthood, characterized by hormonal changes, etc.

adolescents – youths; teenagers

adulteress – woman who has sexual relations outside of marriage

adulterous – pertaining to adultery

aerie – bird's nest; high vantage point

airy – light, fresh, air-filled

ary – any (arch.)

affrayed – caused to be frightened (arch.)

afraid – fearful, frightened

afterward – following; later

afterword – written postscript in a book, essay, etc.; final comment

aid, aide – see *ade*

ail – to be sick

ale – fermented drink, similar to beer

air – (v.) state, express (*a. one's grievances*); expose (*a. one's dirty laundry*) freshen, as linens (w. "out"); (adv.) rumored, under discussion (*in the a.*); (n.) earth's atmosphere; intangible quality, aura (*a. of insouciance*); song, melody

e'er – ever (poetic, arch.)

ere – before

eyre – a circuit, circuit court (ch. Br.)

heir – legatee

airless – close, dank; lacking oxygen   **heirless** – without an heir

aisle – pathway, walkway between seats   **isle** – island

                                                                         I'll – (contr.) I will

all – (adj., adv.) every; in toto; complete/-ly; (n.) totality, sum

                                                                         awl – tool for making holes in wood

allot – mete out, distribute   **a lot** – much, many

allowed – permitted   **aloud** – audible

allusion – reference   **illusion** – mirage

                                                                         (**Aleutian**) – of Alaskan native heritage

altar – holy place   **alter** – change, redo

analyst – one who analyzes; psychoanalyst; specialist in rational thought

                                                                         annalist – one who writes annals; scribe,
                                                                              record-keeper

anchorite – hermit, religious recluse   **ankerite** – Australian mineral similar to
                                                                              dolomite

androgenous – producing only male offspring

                                                                         androgynous – exhibiting both male
                                                                              and female characteristics

annunciation* – in the Bible, Archangel Gabriel's announcement that Mary
would bear the son of God; Catholic church festival celebrating the event

                                                                         enunciation* – precise articulation of
                                                                              vowels and consonants; use of
                                                                              standard pronunciation; specificity,
                                                                              as to terms of an agreement

anser – goose genus   **answer** – (v.) respond; (n.) solution, as
                                                                              to a problem; response

ant – insect   **aunt** – either parent's sister; uncle's wife

ante – stake; poker buy-in   **anti** – against

                                                                         auntie, aunty – aunt; elderly woman

antecedence – precedence; the state of having existed or occurred earlier

                                                                         antecedents – prior existence; logical
                                                                              precedence; referent (in grammar)

---

* "Annunciation" and "enunciation" ideally demonstrate homophonic impre-
cision. Though often pronounced identically, the long "e" of "enunciation"
differentiates the word clearly from "annunciation," with its schwa sound.

apatite – calcium phosphate   **appetite** – hunger, desire, craving

Appalachian – of, from, or pertaining to the Appalachian Mountains or their

residents, culture, flora, fauna, etc.

appellation – name, title, designation

NB: These are "almost" homophones. "Appalachian" usually has a "tch" sound, and a short second "a" as often as long one. But "apple-AY-shun" is a common enough pronunciation to merit entry.

append – add on; attach to   **upend** – turn over; shatter plans by

unexpected changes (*u. negotiations*)

apps – computer software applications **apse** – part of a church, usu. where the

altar is found

arc – part of a circle   **ark** – boat; container for a Torah

arrant – blatant; notorious   **errant** – roving; seeking adventure;

shifting, unreliable (*an e. wind*)

ascent – climb   **assent** – agreement; permission

assistance – help, aid   **assistants** – helpers, aides

ate – consumed; p. tense of *eat*   **eight** – cardinal number after seven

attendance – presence, appearance; total audience, turnout

attendants – assistants, porters;

hangers-on, servants

NB: "Attendants" customarily refers to those providing support or services (e.g., "flight attendants"). For those who show up at an event, "attendees" is customary in modern American usage.

au lait – with milk (*café a.*) (Fr.) **olé** – bravo; well done (Sp.)

Audubon – John J., Haiti-born Amer. naturalist, ornithologist, and painter

autobahn – German highway

auger – drill bit   **augur** – bode, foretell

aught – nothing   **ought** – should; need to

auricle – outer part of the ear   **oracle** – seer, prophet

autarchy – absolute rule; nation ruled by an absolute sovereign

autarky – economic self-sufficiency;

political independence

auteur – creator, writer (Fr.)   **hauteur** – haughtiness, arrogance (Fr.)

aw – expression (*a., shucks*)   **awe** – amazement, wonder

away – distant, not present   **aweigh** – of anchors, clear of the bottom

awful – terrible, dreadful

awn – beard or teasel of grain

axel – ice skating turn

offal – entrails, waste parts of animals

on – atop, over, resting upon

axil – angle formed by a twig or leaf and its branch

axle – rod connecting pairs of wheels

aye – yes; a vote for

eye – (v.) view with interest; ogle; (n.) organ of sight; center of a storm

I – first person singular pronoun

B

baa – ovine sound

bah – exclamation of contempt

babble – (v., n.) prattle; chatter; the sound of water bubbling over stones

babel – cacophony, tumult; place where such confusion reigns (*Tower of B.*); impractical schemes

bach – to live alone as a bachelor

batch – collection, group, bundle

Bach – surname of a family of German composers: Johann Sebastian, Johann Christian, Carl Phillipp Emanuel

bach – (n.) in N.Z., small cottage

bock – dark beer (Ger.), served in spring

Bachs – pl. of "Bach"

balks – hesitates, refuses; thwarts, obstructs; in baseball, begins a pitch but does not throw (giving the one at bat a free base)

bocks – dark German springtime beers

box – (v.) fight w. fists, usu. gloved; hem in constrain (w. "in"); (n.) container, carton

bad – evil, incorrect

bade – instructed, told

Baggie™ – brand of reusable, closable storage bag; any such bag

baggy – sagging, loose

baht – monetary unit of Thailand

bot – robot; an internet application that automatically runs certain tasks; the larva of the botfly

bought – purchased (p. tense of "buy") (fig.) accepted as true

bail – (v.) empty (e.g., water from a boat); (fig.) (w. "out") save, help out; walk out; resign; (n.) payment made to show good faith (legal)

bale – (v., n.)bundle (of) hay, wheat, etc.

bailey – outer wall or court of a castle   bailie – alderman; bailiff (Scot.)

bait(ed) – prepare a fish hook; entice; challenge, usu. w. taunts

bate(d) – hold in abeyance (*with b. breath*)

baize – cloth   bays – inlets; bay trees

bald – hairless   balled – crumpled, rolled into a ball

bawled – cried

ball – orb; dance; good time   bawl – cry, sob uncontrollably

balm – resin; soothing ointment; anything healing (*b. to my soul*)

bomb – (v.) bombard; fail miserably; (n.) explosive ordnance; aerosol dispenser; utter failure

banc – bench, in law courts, w. "en" (*sitting en b.*); judge's seat

bank – (v.) (w. "on") rely, wager; save, set by, build up capital; in billiards, angle a rebounding shot; (n.) cutaway hillside; steep slope; financial institution; any entity for amassing goods in bulk (*sperm b.*)

band – stripe, line; hem, edging; team (*b. of brothers*); instrumental group

banned – prohibited; outlawed

bang – loud noise; explosion; impact   bhang – marijuana (sl.)

bans – prohibits; outlaws   banns – wedding proclamation

bar – (v.) prohibit; (n.) saloon; barrier   barre – handrail (in a dance studio)

bard – poet; troubador; playwright   barred – prohibited, denied (access)

bare – unadorned, plain; nude   bear – (v.) tolerate, carry; (n.) ursine animal; burden (*b. of a job*)

baring – exposing, showing   bearing – (part.) carrying, holding (*load-b. wall*); (n.) carriage, mien

bark – (v.) shout (*b. out orders*); tan w. bark; scrape (a shin); (n.) the sound made by a dog or seal; outer skin of a tree

barque – small boat

base – (v.) establish, build (n.) norm; bottom; inert chemical; political bloc; (n.) foundation; military installation; (adj.) detestable, odious, immoral

bass – (n., adj.) deepest musical range (*b. voice*); bass guitar or cello

based – located, established

baste – moisten (in cooking); stitch, sew w. loose, temporary stitches; beat, thrash

bases – v. sing., n. pl., of "base"

basis – supporting factor; principle, theory

basest – lowest, most despicable

bassist – player of a double bass

bask – sunbathe; preen oneself in response to praise

basque – bodice, tunic, usu. tight-fitting

Basque – (n.) ethno-cultural group of the W. Pyrenees; (adj.) related to their language, history, culture

bat – (v.) hit w. a bat; (fig.) casually consider (*b. around*); toss; (n.) flying mammal, order *Chiroptera*; in cricket or baseball, club for hitting balls; stout stick

batt – layer of fabric; felted cotton

Bataan – Philippine peninsula

baton – staff; conductor's stick

bauble – trinket, adornment

bobble – bounce, dangle, float

baud – unit of electronic speed in telegraphy and computing

bawd – loose woman, prostitute

bay – (v.) corner, entrap; (n.) inlet, alcove; reddish color, as of a horse

bey – Turkish semi-royal title

bazaar – market, agora, fair

bizarre – strange, odd

NB: These are "almost," not precise, homophones.

be – exist

bee – flying insect; contest (*spelling b.*); nagging idea (*b. in one's bonnet*)

beach – (v.) land a boat on shore; abandon; ground, strand, as a whale; (n.) shore; sandy seaside, used for sunbathing

beech – any of a genus of deciduous trees

bead – aim; drilled ornament

Bede – English historian, 672-735 (*the Venerable B.*)

beat – (v..) hit repeatedly; win; overcome (*b. the odds*); (n.) rhythm

beet – a red root vegetable

beau – boyfriend; counterpart to *belle*   **bow** – weapon that shoots arrows; device to vibrate strings of violins, etc. (see also *bough*, *bow*)

beaut – prime example   **butte** – rock formation

been – p. part. of "be"   **bin** – container, usu. open, for storage; trashcan (Br.)

beer – beverage brewed of grain, barley, etc., and hops; similar nonalcoholic beverages (*root b.*)

bier – platform for a coffin; beer (Ger.), viz. "biergarten" (pub or café, usu. outdoors)

bell – chime; instrument   **belle** – beautiful woman; siren

belligerence – fighting spirit, aggression; antagonism

belligerents – opponents; enemies

berg – iceberg   **burg** – (sl.) town, hamlet

berry – fruit   **bury** – inter; (fig.) hide, conceal

berth – bed, as in a ship or train   **birth** – origin, start; arrival of new life

bet – wager   **bête** – beast (Fr.); w. "noire," irritant; something hated or feared

better – improved   **bettor** – one who bets; gambler

(**betters**) (n., pl.) social superiors

bib – protective napkin   **Bibb** – variety of lettuce

bibb – nautical bracket

bidders – buyers at an auction   **bitters** – an herbal alcohol

bight – loop, bend; riverbend   **bite** – (v.) grip with teeth; sting; (n.) morsel; snack

byte – group of binary digits (bits)

billed – named, credited, as entertainers; having a beak or nib

build – erect, construct

bird – any member of the class *Aves*; vulgar extension of the middle finger to express contempt (*flip the b.*)

burred – spoke w. a Scottish accent

"The difference between the almost right word and the right word is really a large matter—'tis the difference between the lightning-bug and the lightning."
—Mark Twain

birl – roll logs with the feet   **burl** – pattern of some woodgrains

bit – (v.) p. tense of "bite"; (n.) small amount; part of a bridle placed in a horse's mouth; single digit in binary systems in computing, part of a byte; sharp, part of a drill or brace that drills holes

    bitt – post on a ship's deck, cf. bollard

blew – exhaled strongly; stormed windily; wasted, lost unexpectedly (*b. a big lead*)

    blue – (n.) color ranging from cyan to midnight; (fig.) sky, heavens; (adj.) describing such color; sad, depressed

bloc – political group; voting alliance   **block** – (v.) obstruct; (n.) solid piece of any material; obstruction; oblong building unit (*concrete b.*); pulley system (*b. and tackle*)

blond – fair, light-colored (of skin or hair); with a pale finish (of furniture, wood)

    blonde – (n.) woman or girl with fair, flaxen hair; (fig., sl.) low-intellect or easily confused woman (*dizzy b.*); (adj.) of females, fair-haired

boar – wild pig   **bore** – (v.) drill into; tire; (n.) hole made by drilling (*b. hole*); state of boredom (*what a b.*); tedious person

board – (v.) rent rooms with meals; (n.) wooden plank; meals (*room & b.*)

    bored – (v.) drilled, as a hole; caused to lose interest; (adj.) uninterested, overcome by tedium

boarder – renter, roomer   **border** – edge; perimeter

boatswain – warrant officer on ships who supervises crews and their tasks

    boson – a subatomic particle

    bosun – alt. sp. of "boatswain"

bocks – see *Bachs*

bode – presage; serve as an omen; predict   **bowed** – bent, curved in an arc

bold – courageous, forward   **bowled** – stunned (*b. over*); played at the game of bowling; threw the ball toward the batsman in cricket

bolder – more forward, daring

boulder – large rock, stone

bole – trunk of a tree; stem

boll – tuft of cotton

bowl – (v.) stun (*b. over*); play at bowls; pitch at cricket (n.) round, deep dish for serving soup, cereal, ice cream, etc.

bollix – bungle, botch (usu. w. "up")

bollocks – (n.) testicles; (interj.) baloney, nonsense (ch. Br.)

boos – pl. of "boo"; catcalls

booze – alcohol, liquor (sl.)

bootie – infant's footwear, usu. knitted

booty – loot, as from a pirate raid

born – given birth

borne – carried

borough – government division; township, county (also boro)

burro – ass, donkey

burrow – (v.) tunnel underground; nestle (*b. under the covers*); (n.) underground den for moles, etc.

bough – tree limb

bow – (v.) bend at the waist in greeting or thanks; (n.) front of a ship

bouillon – stock; thin soup

bullion – ingots of gold, silver, etc.

box – see *Bachs*

boy – male child

buoy – floating marker in a sea or lake

brae – hill, slope (Scot.)

bray – (v.) make the sound of a donkey; neigh; laugh harshly; pulverize, as in a mortar; turn to powder; spread thin, as ink; (n.) sound made by a donkey (fig.) loud, off-key singing

braes – hills (Scot.)

braise – sear, char, cook

brays – 3rd p. sing. form of "bray"

braid – (v.) plait, weave; (n.) a section of hair or rope plaited into a woven pattern

brayed – p. tense of "bray"

brake – (v.) slow a vehicle; (n.) mechanism for reducing speed; stand of shrubs; planted field (*cane b.*)

break – (v.) shatter; separate; (n.) rest, pause in action; division into parts

braking – slowing, decelerating

breaking – shattering; the collapsing of a wave as it approaches the shore

brassie – No. 2 wood, in golf (arch.)   **brassy** – made of brass; loud, blaring
                                              brazen, impudent; cheap, showy

breach – (v.) break through; leap out of water, as a whale; (n.) infraction;
                                              opening, as in military defenses

                                              breech – rump; baby born buttocks first;
                                              back end of a gun barrel; (pl.) trousers

bread – staple food of flour, water, and yeast (*our daily b.*); money, cash (sl.)

                                              bred – raised, reared

bree – thin, watery broth (Scot.)   **brie** – soft French cheese

brewed – distilled (as tea); concocted; (fig.) came up with (a plan)

                                              brood – (v.) worry; mate; incubate (eggs);
                                              (n.) chicks; (fig.) family, children

brews – (v.) distills, prepares; (n.) decoctions, drinks; (fig.) beers

                                              bruise – (v.) injure, cause a blemish to
                                              skin, fruit, etc.; (n.) discoloration
                                              resulting from such an injury

bridal – relating to a bride or wedding   **bridle** – (v.) bristle, show resentment;
                                              (n.) part of a horse's headgear

brilliance – éclat; high intelligence; genius **brilliants** – gemstones cut in an oval
                                              shape; ring containing such a stone

broach – open, instigate   **brooch** – decorative pin, often jewelled

broom – implement for sweeping; plant whose twigs are used for such a purpose

                                              brume – fog, mist

brows – eyebrows   **browse** – read, scan, glance at

bruit – (v.) spread a rumor; (n.) rumor   **brut** – very dry, as champagne

                                              brute – (n.) rough, coarse person; boor;
                                              (adj.) savage; insensate; inhuman

buccal – of or toward the cheek   **buckle** – (v.) fasten a belt, shoe, etc.;
                                              (n.) metal clasp for a belt, shoe, etc.

Buncombe – county in western NC   **bunkum** – hogwash; tall tales

bur – spiny casing of certain seeds, e.g., chestnut, cocklebur

                                              burr – (v.) roughen an edge; speak
                                              w. a burr; (n.) trilled "r" of Scot.
                                              dialect; rough edge on a disc, etc.

                                              brrr – exclam. indicating "It's cold."

burger – meat sandwich; hamburger

burley – variety of tobacco

bus/es – vehicle(s)

burgher – villager; town citizen (Ger.)

burly – strong, heavy; massive

buss/es – kiss(es)

NB: Newspapers often write "busses" and "bussed" for "buses" and "bused." Just remember that "busses," like "kisses," takes two (esses).

bused – traveled by bus

but – except, save for

buy – purchase

buyer – purchaser

bussed – kissed

bust – (v.) break (irr.); (adj.) bankrupt (sl.); (n.) sculpted head; bosom

butt – barrel; object of a joke; stub of a cigar or cigarette; derrière, buttocks

by – (adv.) near, adjacent to; (prep.) beside, next to; indicating authorship

bye – special bonus; free pass, privilege

'bye – farewell; goodbye

byre – barn for cattle

C

cache – stash, hiding place

cachou – lozenge, usu. licorice-flavored

caddie – (v.) provide clubs, balls, etc. in golf; (n.) golfer's assistant

cash – (v.) redeem, as a check; (fig.) die (*c. it in*); (n.) currency, paper money; coin, specie

cashew – tropical evergreen producing oils used in resins and plastics; the nut of the tree, edible only after cooking

caddy – tray for serving tea

caecilian – (n., adj.) wormlike amphibian

Cain – son of Adam & Eve (bibl.); (fig.) anger, havoc (*raise c.*)

caird – tinker, gypsy

Sicilian – from or of Sicily

cane – marsh grass; walking stick

cared – loved, cherished; felt concern or responsibility for

calendar – system of plotting days and dates; chart or scheme displaying such a system; docket, list of appointments

calender – (v.) squeeze paper through paired cylinders; (n.) the machine for finishing paper in such a fashion

calix – chalice (alt. pronunciation)   **calyx** – sepal; set of protective leaves
                                                                    surrounding a flower or bud

calk – metal plate (horseshoe)   **caulk** – (v.) seal, make waterproof; (n.)
                                                                    putty, sealant

call – (v.) shout; reach by telephone; (n.) decision; inner direction, esp. religious

                                                            caul – membrane enclosing a fetus

caller – user of a telephone; visitor (*gentleman c.*) (arch.)

                                                            choler – ire, anger; bad temper

                                                            collar – (v.) arrest; (n.) part of a shirt or
                                                                    harness that surrounds the neck

callous – unfeeling; pitiless   **callus** – hard, thickened skin

came – arrived, attended; ejaculated (sl.) **kame** – gravelly glacial hillock (Br. dial.)

cannon – large, mounted gun   **canon** – body of law; church law; author's
                                                                    works; contrapuntal musical structure

cant – jargon; insincere piety; slant; beveled edge; outside angle (of a building);

                                                            can't – (conj.) cannot; may not

canter – fast gait, trot   **cantor** – singer; song leader in a
                                                                    church or synagogue

canvas – cotton or linen fabric; sails; cloth prepared for oil painting

                                                            canvass – (v., n.) survey or solicit votes

capital – (adj.) extremely important; first-rate (*a c. idea*); punishable by death (*c.*
                                                                    offense); (n.) uppercase letter; seat of
                                                                    government; top of a column;
                                                                    available principal; accumulated
                                                                    wealth or value (*political c.*)

                                                            capitol – building housing a state or
                                                                    national legislature (*state c.*)

capo – head of a mafia crime family   **kapo** – in Nazi concentration camps, a
                                                                    prisoner assigned to supervise others

   NB: Capo, pronounced with a long "a," is the device placed over the strings
of a guitar to change the key.

carat – unit of gem weight   **caret** – mark (^) used in editing

                                                            carrot – root vegetable

                                                            karat – measure of the purity of gold

caries – dental decay   **carries** – totes; bears a burden; drives

carol – song; Christmas tune   **carrel** – reading desk in a library

carpal – (n.) one of the bones of the carpus (adj.) of the carpus bones

carpel – pistil; fem. part of a plant

cask – round barrel, usu. of wood, for maturing or storing wine, liquor, sherry, etc.; keg, tun

casque – visorless medieval helmet; enlarged upper bill on some birds

cast – (v.) throw, toss; make a casting of; assign actors to roles; limn, describe; (n.) model, copy; company of actors in a play; sheath to protect a broken limb

caste – class, social status

caster – ball on furniture legs to allow it to roll; one who casts; cruet

castor – beaver gland extract used as a lure; type of bean or extract

Castor – Greek deity; with Pollux, one of two stars in the constellation Gemini

caudal – at or near a tail   **caudle** – warm, medicinal beverage

coddle – treat gently; soft-boil eggs

caught – snared, trapped; discovered (*c. in the act*); arrested

cot – camp bed, usu. portable

cause – origin, impetus   **caws** – sounds made by crows

cay – small, sandy reef island   **key** – implement used to open a lock; answer to a puzzle; one of an array of symbols on a computer keyboard

quay – wharf (also pron. "kay")

cedar – evergreen tree; wood of that tree   **seeder** – device for spreading seeds

cede – give up (a claim to)   **seed** – germ of a living thing; origin

ceiling – upper limit; inside top of a room; visibility under clouds

sealing – closing securely, making inaccessible; locking away

cell – zygote; smallest unit of life capable of reproducing; monk's room; prison enclosure; cabal, group of zealots

sell – exchange for money; retail; convince (*s. an idea*)

cellar – basement   **seller** – vendor, retailer

cense – spread incense	cents, scents (see *cent*)
	sense – (v.) feel, intuit; (n.) wisdom, rationality (*common s.*); physical ability such as touch, sight, smell; special ability, e.g., ESP (*sixth s.*)
censer – incense holder; thurible	censor – official overseer of print or other expression of ideas; bowdlerizer
	sensor – device to detect heat, smoke, motion, etc.
cent – one-penny coin	scent – aroma; trace, hint
	sent – dispatched; mailed
cercus – abdominal antenna on insects	circus – raree show, usu. w. clowns, acrobats, animals, exhibits, etc.; roundabout (ch. Br.) (*Picadilly C.*)
cereal – grain; grain food	serial – in a series, part of a group
Ceres – Greek goddess of the harvest	series – group or collection in successive order
cession – formal ceding of rights	session – meeting, scheduled period
cetaceous – of whales, dolphins, and other sea mammals	
	setaceous – having bristles
Cezanne – French painter	saison – season (Fr.)
	seize ans – sixteen years (Fr.)

NB: These are not homophones in French, but English speakers often do not differentiate among the nuances of their pronunciation.

chaise – long reclining chair (Fr.)	shays – wagons, carriages
chalk – powdery mineral	chock – (adj.) completely (*c.-full*); (n.) blocker, brake (*wheel-c.*)
champagne – a type of sparkling wine from the Champagne region of France	
	Champaign – a city and county in east-central Illinois
chance – (v.) risk, dare; (n.) happenstance, randomness; opportunity	
	chants – (v.) intones; (n.) repeated rhythmic phrases, usu. sung in unison
chantey – rhythmic sailor's song, trad. used to maintain rhythm while rowing	
	shanty – hovel; shabby dwelling

chard – edible leafy vegetable

chary – wary, skeptical

chased – followed, ran after; embossed

chatelain – keeper of a castle

charred – seared; burned

cherry – tree; fruit of that tree

chaste – pure, undefiled; virginal

chatelaine – mistress of a castle; chain on which are kept keys, purse, etc.

cheap – inexpensive; frugal

cheep – sound of a bird or chick

check – (v.) hold, rein in; review for accuracy, confirm; see to; (n.) limit; financial draft; payment (as in *paycheck*)

cheque – alt. of "check" (chiefly Br.)

Czech – of a Slavic people, culture, language, history, or nation

chews – masticates; mulls over, ponders (w. "on"); obsesses over

choose – opt for; decide on; elect

chez – at the home of (Fr.)

Chile – nation in S. America

shay – horse-drawn buggy; carriage

chili – hot pepper; food or sauce, usu. of meat, made with chilis

chilly – uncomfortably cool; not warm; emotionally distant

chitin – hard, secreted shell of insects, mollusks, etc.

chiton – long garment worn by women in ancient Greece; class of mollusks

choir – choral group; church singers; (fig.) supporters (*preach to the c.*)

quire – 1/20th of a ream (25 sheets)

choler – ire, anger; angry temperament

collar – (v.) seize, arrest; (n.) part of a garment or harness that surrounds the neck; sleeve over a pipe, etc.

choral – of a singing group

coral – (n.) skeletal reef structure; (adj.) burnt orange color

chorale – genre of vocal music, often devotional; singing group

corral – (v.) gather together, hem in; (n.) pen for animals

chord – group of musical tones

cord – rope; anat. structure in the throat (*vocal c.*); measure of wood

cored – removed the center (fruit); took a sample of (a tree, ice, etc.)

chough – crow-like European blackbird **chuff** – boor; rude person

chow – food; meal; (Chow) dog breed **ciao** – good-bye (It.)

chute – channel, sluice **shoot** – (v.) traverse at speed (*s. the rapids*); discharge a weapon; (n.) photographic session; (interj.) exclam. of chagrin

cite – name as a source; refer to **sight** – view, range; visual sense

site – location

clabbered – curdled, as milk **clapboard** – wooden boards used as siding in construction

clack – (v.) make a sound like poultry; chatter; (n.) such a sound

claque – a group paid to applaud a performance; devoted fans

clan – family or tribal group **Klan** – white power group Ku Klux Klan

Claus – Ger. name "Klaus," usu. Claus for St. Nicholas (Santa Claus)

clause – verbal phrase comprising a subject and verb; section of a contract

claws – (v.) scratches; tears, using talons or nails; clings (to), grasps (at); (n.) sharpened nails on animals' paws

cleek – hook; nine-iron (Scot.) **clique** – coterie; "in" group (see *click*)

NB: A French word, "clique" is properly pronounced "kleek"; the pronunciation "click" is now accepted in most dictionaries.

Cleo – female name (Cleopatra) **Clio** – American advertising award

clew – ball of thread; lower corner of a square sail (naut.)

clue – hint, suggestion; fact or object leading to the solution to a mystery

click – (v.) jibe, fall into place, make understood; (n.) brief, sharp sound, as of a door closing

clique – coterie; exclusive group

climb – (v.) ascend; (n.) ascent **clime** – climate, atmosphere; region

coal – carbonate fuel **koel** – cuckoo of India, Australia

kohl – dark blue or black cosmetic application; type of makeup

coarse – rude, unrefined **course** – pathway, direction; ongoing stages of development

coat – (v.) apply paint, etc.; (n.) layer of paint, fur, etc.; outer clothing

cote – shelter for fowl, sheep, etc.

côte – coastal area (Fr.) (*C. d'Azur*)

cob – male swan; small horse; core of an ear of corn, to which kernels adhere

Cobb – American salad of iceberg lettuce, bacon, chicken, hard-boiled eggs, avocado, and Roquefort cheese

kob – orange-red antelope

cocks – roosters; penises (sl., vulgar)   **cox** – lead at crew; act as coxswain

coco – coconut palm; its fruit   **cocoa** – powder made from cacao seeds; sweet beverage made with such powder and sugar

coded – in code; secret   **coated** – covered by; painted over

coeur – heart (Fr.)   **cur** – dog, usu. derogatory

coffer – box for valuables; crate, chest   **cougher** – one who coughs

coif – hairdo   **quaff** – (v. n.) drink, sip

coir – fiber of a coconut husk, prepared for use in ropemaking

coyer – more demure; suggestively flirtatious, coquettish

cola – tree whose caffeine-rich fruit is used to make sweet, carbonated drinks

kola – the nut or fruit of the cola tree

(colicky) – nauseated, esp. infants   **(colloquy)** – dialogue; discussion

collard – leafy, edible green   **collared** – arrested; wearing a collar

colonel – military rank immediately below brigadier general

kernel – seed, heart; edible part

color – (v.) dye, tint; fill in pictures in a coloring book; blush; describe, usu. w. bias; (n.) any primary hue (red, blue, or yellow) or mixture thereof; (fig.) nature, atmosphere, composition of a group or its participants

culler – one who culls; gleaner

comedy – funny play; joke   **comity** – civility, politeness

complacence – contentment; self-satisfaction; smugness (also "complacency")

complaisance – willingness to please

complement – match, fit   **compliment** – praise, salute

con – (v.) swindle; (n.) convict, felon; crook; (adj.) anti; opposed to

       conn – steer, as a ship

       kahn – title used in Mongolia, Iran, etc.

conceded – resigned; admitted defeat **conceited** – vain, egotistic

conch – large, edible mussel; its shell; (colloq.) long-time resident or native of

       the Florida Keys

       conk – (v.) hit on the head; knock out;

        w. "out," die; fail suddenly; (n.) head;

        nose; blow to the head (ch. Brit.);

        fungal disease affecting trees and bark

confectionary – of a confectioner's work **confectionery** – candy shop; sweetshop

conker – horse-chestnut; children's game using their shells

       conquer – overcome an enemy; defeat

consonance – agreement; harmony **consonants** – speech sounds that stop

       or slow the passage of air; non-vowels

Constance – woman's name; alt. sp. of constancy

       constants – unchanging things; in math,

        quantities whose value is unvarying

continence – self-restraint; moderation; sexual chastity; control of one's

       bowels despite disabling ailments

       continents – earth's seven major land

       masses

convalescence – period or state of recuperation from illness

       convalescents – those in recuperation

coo – make sounds like a dove; romance someone with soft words (*bill and c.*)

       coup – overthrow of a government, oft.

        by military force; putsch; surprise

        victory, as in Bridge or other games

coolie – unskilled laborer, trad. in China **coulee** – deep, seasonally dry gully;

       stream of lava

coop – (v.) confine, pen (w. "up"); (n.) roosting house for pigeons

       coupe – two-door automobile (orig. Fr.,

        coupé, pron. cou-PAY)

cops – (v.) accepts a plea bargain; (w. "to") admits; (n.) police officers (sl.)

       copse – stand of trees; thicket

copyright – registered authorship, proprietorship; creative origination

> **copywrite(r)** – writer of advertising materials; commercial writer

coquet – flirt; trifle with   **coquette** – a woman who flirts

core – center, heart   **corps** – military unit; group

correspondence – equivalency, similarity; exchange of letters

> **correspondents** – reporters, journalists; those with whom one exchanges letters

cosign – add one's signature to a document; guarantee another's loan

> **cosine** – a ratio in trigonometry

council – assembly; body of elected or appointed officials

> **counsel** – (v.) advise; (n.) advice; attorney

courier – messenger   **currier** – dresser or finisher of leather

> **Currier** – Nathaniel, 19th-century Am. lithographer and printmaker (*C. & Ives*)

cousin – kinsman; offspring of a parent's sibling; (fig.) something similar

> **cozen** – cheat, swindle

coward – one without courage   **cowered** – hid in fear; cringed

coy – bashful, shy; coquettish   **koi** – goldfish

craft – folk art; skill; witchcraft, knowledge of Wiccan practices

> **kraft** – brown, coated wrapping paper

crape – alt. sp. of "crepe"; mourning garb; w. "myrtle," an ornamental shrub

> **crepe** – crinkled silk or rayon cloth
> (**crêpe**) – (Fr.) thin pancake, usu. rolled and stuffed with filling

crappie – a variety of Amer. sunfish   **crappy** – cheap, lousy; worthless (sl.)

crate – box, carton   **krait** – snake of SE Asia

crawl – (v.) move on hands and knees; move slowly; (n.) very slow movement

> **kraal** – enclosed village in S. Africa; stockade, corral for livestock

creak – (v.) squeak; move with difficulty; (n.) harsh or shrill sound

> **creek** – small stream, rill
> **Creek** – American Indian nation

Cretan – one from Crete   **cretin** – dolt, idiot, moron

crew – (v.) row; operate a plane or boat under a captain; (n.) rowing team;
group of sailors, fliers, etc.

cru – of grapes and wine, harvest

crewel – embroidery yarn   cruel – harsh, unkind; sadistic

crews – (v.) rows; operates a plane or boat under a captain; (n.) teams doing
such work

cruise – (v.) travel easily (*c. along*); go by
sea; survey a crowd seeking pick-up
partners (sl.); (n.) vacation aboard ship

cruse – container for liquids; cruet

croc – crocodile (sl.)   crock – earthenware pot; shard; old,
broken-down person, horse, etc.;
baloney, nonsense (*that's a c.*)

crumby – full of crumbs   crummy – cheap, inferior; disgusting

cubical – shaped like a cube   cubicle – small office workspace

cue – hint, signal; pool stick   Kew – public garden in London, Eng.

queue – line of people (chiefly Br.)

curdle – go bad, sour   kirtle – short tunic; skirt

currant – a fruit of a seedless grape   current – (n.) flow of water or electricity;
strength of such flow; (adj.) of the
present time; contemporary (*c. events*)

curser – one who curses   cursor – electronic caret; pointer on a
computer indicating position for
typing, design, etc.

cyc – (abbr.) cyclorama; theater curtain used as backdrop for stage settings

psych – (v.) w. "out," manipulate; trick;
(n.) psychology; (adj.) psychological,
psychiatric (sl.) (*p. ward*)

cygnet – young swan   signet – seal, official mark

cymbal – percussion instrument of brass, usu. used in pairs

symbol – image, representation

cypress – evergreen tree prized for its wood; wood of that tree

Cyprus – Mediterranean island nation

In English, echo phrases always place "i" before "a": bric-a-brac, fiddle-faddle,
kit-kat, knick-knack, mish-mash, rip-rap, tic-tac-toe, zig-zag.

D

dairy – (n.) a farm producing milk, usu. from cattle or goats; (adj.) pertaining to dairying; describing a category of foods in Jewish Kosher law

Derry – a seaport in N. Ireland

Dali – Salvador, Sp. artist (1904-89)   **dolly** – wheeled cart; doll (dim.)

dam – (v.) shut off, stem, block, as water; (n.) structure to hold back water; ewe; wife (colloq.)

damn – (v.) condemn, curse; (exclam.) drat; darn it

dammed – blocked, esp. water; checked; held in abeyance

damned – (v.) cursed, condemned to hell; (adj.) beyond redemption

Dane – person from Denmark; breed of dog (*Great D.*)

deign – condescend; stoop to

dawn – (v.) begin, arise; (with "on") become aware of; (n.) sunrise, daybreak

don – (v.) put on, wear; (n.) teacher at Br. universitiess; traditionally, It. nobleman (*D. Carlo*); Mafia leader

day – 24-hour period marking a complete rotation of Earth; hours of light

dey – pasha; formerly, gov. of Algiers

days – pl. of "day"   **daze** – (v.) stun; bewilder; (n.) stupor

deys – pl. of "dey"

dear – cherished, beloved   **deer** – ruminant of the family *Cervidae*; buck, doe, fawn, stag, etc.

dense – thick; mentally slow, stupid   **dents** – small hollow in metal, made by a blow; lessening, easing, minimizing by an effort (*make a d.*)

dental – of the teeth   **dentil** – one of a series of small blocks below the cornice of a building

dependence – condition of being dependent; reliance; subordination

dependents – those supported by another; subordinates

descent – downward movement; slope; disintegration; lowering

dissent – (v., n.) disagree(ment)

desert – abandon, leave behind   **dessert** – final, usu. sweet, course of a
                                                                          meal; (fig., pl.) come-uppance (*just
                                                                          desserts*)

NB: "Just desserts" may be derived from "deserves" rather than "dessert."

desperate – hopeless, extreme   **disparate** – ill-assorted; distinct

deterrence – plan or arrangement to avoid an outcome; such a condition

                                                              deterrents – conditions or actions that
                                                                          will serve to deter

deuce – the two in a deck of cards   **douce** – sweet, pleasant; hospitable

deviance – deviation from a norm; behavior considered deviant; perversion

                                                              deviants – (n., pl.) people who engage
                                                                          in perverse, inappropriate, or
                                                                          sexually offensive behavior

dew – condensation; mist   **due** – owed

                                                              (**do**) – (v.) undertake, accomplish; (n.)
                                                                          hairstyle (sl.)

NB: "Dew" and "due" (but not "do") may be pronounced "dyoo" or "doo."

dewed – became wet with dew   **dude** – overly fashionable youth; dandy, fop
dews – pl. of "dew"   **dos** – approved actions (*d. and don'ts*)

                                                              dues – membership fees or payments

dhole – wild dog of S. Asia   **dole** – (v.) mete out; allot; (n.) public
                                                                          welfare (*on the d.*)

dhow – a ship of the Indian ocean   **tao** – Taoism; Chinese philosophy of
                                                                          simplicity and selflessness

NB: Though "tao" is properly pronounced with an initial "d," Westerners
most often pronounce it with a "t" to rhyme with the Greek letter "tau."

dhows – ship of the Indian ocean   **douse** – soak, put out (a fire)

                                                              dowse – seek water underground using
                                                                          a special tool or stick (colloq.)

NB: The "s" of "dowse" is sybilant, unlike the "z" of the primary words,
but many people do not differentiate their pronunciation.

diarist – one who keeps a diary or journal; recorder of daily events

                                                              direst – most dangerous, extreme
dicker – bargain, haggle   **duiker** – antelope of Africa

dickey – false shirt front, bib; small bird   **dicky** – unsound, as a heart (colloq. Br.)

die – (v.) expire; end; (n.) marked cube for gambling; form used to stamp or cut machine parts

dye – (v.) color; (n.) liquid for tinting

died – passed away, expired   **dyed** – tinted, colored

dike – ditch; embankment, dam   **dyke** – (n.) lesbian (sl.)

dine – sup; eat elegantly   **dyne** – measure of force

dire – dangerous; last-ditch   **dyer** – one who applies dyes

disburse – pay out; spend   **disperse** – depart; scatter

disc – record, electronic recording   **disk** – flat, round object, as a coin; (fig.) any similar shape, as the moon

discreet – modest, self-effacing; secret   **discrete** – separate, unrelated

discussed – spoke about   **disgust** – (v.) offend, shock; (n.) aversion, strong distaste

dissidence – disagreement; objection   **dissidents** – those objecting; outsiders

dits – pl. of "dit," used in Morse code to indicate short signals

ditz – airhead; empty-headed woman

divorcé – divorced man   **divorcée** – divorced woman

djinn – genie; magician   **gin** – (v.) (w. "up") energize; (n.) card game; liquor distilled from corn and barley; engine (*cotton g.*)

do – trad. first musical note (*do-re-mi...*)   **doe** – female deer

dough – mix of flour, water, eggs, etc. for baking; money (sl.)

doc – physician, veterinarian (sl.); document (abbr., sl.)

dock – pier, berth, quay

does (n., pl.) female deer   **doughs** – baking mixtures

doze – sleep, nap

Visualizing similar words with strikingly different images can help you remember which is which. For example, you might envision a lady from *Maine* with a *mane* of hair that was the *main* attribute of her beauty. Or think of a play*wright* who will *write* about a church that always uses the *right rite* for a ceremonial event.

Broadway composer Stephen Sondheim, a master of rhyme, rhythm, puns, double entendres, and other forms of creative word use, wrote a memorable line in his musical *Into the Woods* about Jack (of Beanstalk fame) and his poor old cow, getting older, no longer giving milk, "while her withers wither with her."

done – finished, complete   **dun** – (v.) demand money owed for a
debt; (adj.) tan, neutral in color

donjon – castle keep; stronghold; inner, fortified tower of a castle; prison (arch.)

dungeon – prison, oft. below ground

dour – glum, unhappy   **dower** – dowry

draft – (v.) enlist, call upon; register for (usu. compulsory) military service; draw,
sketch; write; tap, as beer; pull a load,
usu. by oxen, horses, etc.; (n.) system
to ensure compulsory registration (as
for military service); prelim. drawing
or writing; liquid from a spigot; air
current from a loose door or window;
payment from a financial institution;
check; (adj.) referring to the above (*D.
Board, d. document, d. horse, d. beer*)

draught – draft (ch. Brit.)

drafts – (v., n.) pl. of "draft"   **draughts** – game of checkers (Brit.)

drier – more arid   **dryer** – machine for drying clothes

dual – in two parts; paired   **duel** – (v., n.) formal challenge fight w.
swords or guns; (fig.) test of skill

ducked – evaded, dropped or moved to avoid (a blow, bullet, etc.)

duct – tube or passageway for carrying
air, water, etc.

dyeing – tinting, coloring, as cloth   **dying** – expiring, moribund

E

earn – merit, work for; deserve   **ern** or **erne** – sea bird

urn – vase, usu. ornate; appliance for
brewing coffee; samovar

eaten – p. part. of "eat"; consumed; eroded; rusted

Eton – town in Buckinghamshire, Eng.;
boys' preparatory school in the town;
collar or jacket worn by its students

eave – overhanging part of a roof   **eve** – evening; night before

eek – sound of fright or surprise   **eke** – make use of limited resources

eerie – strange, uncanny, hinting of the supernatural; macabre

> **Erie** – one of the Great Lakes; also a NY canal Penn. city and county

effluence – emanation; a flowing out, of a pipe, sewer, etc.

> **effluents** – outflows; what flows out of a pipe, etc., usu. impure

el – in Chicago, an elevated train

> **ell** – right-angled building addition or pipe joint; unit of measure (45 in.)

> **Elle** – French fashion magazine

emery – abrasive mineral, often used for filing (nails, etc.)

> **Emory** – university in Atlanta, Ga.

entrance – way in, entry; access

> **entrants** – those enrolling, signing up, entering a contest

enumerable – countable; separate, subject to individual listing

> **innumerable** – countless; infinite

NB: Only slightly different in sound, but virtually opposite in meaning, these two words can be easily mistaken in spoken English.

equivalence – relative equality, of size, dimension, other measure

> **equivalents** – (n.) qualities of similar value; (adj.) equal in value, weight, etc.

err – make a mistake

> **er** – (interj.) (ch. Br.) uh, um; ahem

NB: Americans have generally adopted the pronunciation "air" for "err," probably to match the sound of "error." "Ur" is the traditional pronunciation.

errant – roving, adventurous; (*knight e.*) shifting, unreliable (*an e. wind*)

> **arrant** – blatant, notorious

Esther – woman's name; in the Bible, Jewish queen of Persian king Ahasuerus

> **ester** – aromatic chemical extract

estrous – (adj.) of or pertaining to the female reproductive cycle; ovulating

> **estrus** – (n.) cycle of ovulation in many female animals

Ethel – woman's name

> **ethyl** – a monovalent radical, C_2H_5

ewe – female sheep

> **you** – (pron.) second person singular; thou

> **yew** – tree or shrub of genus *Taxus*; wood of the tree, often used in making baseball bats

exercise – (v., n.) work out; tone up   **exorcise** – remove demons

expedience – convenience; self-interest; practical wisdom

expedients – rationales; justifications

every day (adv.) quotidian; daily; (n.) each 24-hour period marking a complete rotation of the earth

everyday – (adj.) mundane, typical; not out of the ordinary

eye – (v.) view with interest; ogle; (n.) organ of sight; taste, attraction (*an e. for beauty*); intuition; storm center

aye – yes; a vote in favor

I – (pron.) first person singular

eyed – observed; ogled   **I'd** – (contr.) I would; I had

eyelet – in sewing or embroidery, small opening in a needle for lace or thread; loophole, grommet

islet – small island; cay

F

faerie – magical land of elves and fairies **fairy** – magical being, sprite, pixie; effeminate gay man, homosexual (sl.)

ferry – (v.) transport people, goods, livestock, usu. across a body of water; (n.) boat used for ferrying

fain – (adj.) glad, eager (arch.); (adv.) gladly, eagerly

fane – temple, church building (arch.); (fig.) sanctuary

feign – pretend

faint – (v.) collapse, swoon; fall into oblivion; (adj.) weak, barely noticeable; scornful (*f. praise*)

feint – false punch, jab; ploy, ruse

fair – (n.) exposition; market; public party; (adj.) mediocre, average

fare – (v.) go, turn out (*f. well*) (n.) food, sustenance; entertainment program; price, fee; paying passenger

fairing – gift; casing designed to reduce aeronautic drag

faring – (v.) succeeding; (n.) trek, journey

faro – card game

Faeroe or Faroe – group of Danish islands in the N. Atlantic

farro – the grain of an ancient wheat with tightly encloses kernels

farrow – (v.) bear a litter of pigs; (n.) shoat; litter (obs.); of cattle, barren

(Pharaoh) – king of ancient Egypt

NB: These words are not quite homophones but are often pronounced identically. But however similar the spoken words, what matters in the written language is to use the correct word.

fat – (n.) insulating body tissue in mammals, fish, birds; grease or lard derived therefrom; unhealthful excess of such tissue; (adj.) obese; robust (*f. paycheck*)

phat – excellent; top-notch (Amer. sl.)

fate – destiny; outcome

(fête) – (v.) honor, celebrate; (n.) gala

fait (w. "accompli") – (Fr.) done deal

faun – mythical deity w. human head and torso and goat's body; satyr; enticing, often adrogynous creature

fawn – (v.) dote; (n.) baby deer; (adj.) of the color of a fawn; pale tan

faux – false; pretend

foe – enemy

faze – disturb, bother, upset

phase – stage, step; visible aspect of the moon

feat – deed; accomplishment

feet – pl. of "foot"; measure of distance

fern – nonflowering plant that propagates by spores

firn – granular snow found on glaciers

fessed – (sl.) confessed, admitted

fest – festival, carnival; celebration

feudal – of a medieval European system of government, based on ownership of land by overlords, w. labor provided by serfs

futile – pointless; ineffective

fiancé – man affianced to marry

fiancée – woman affianced to marry

file – (v.) organize, place with like items; (n.) folder to hold papers; cabinet for such folders; rasp, emery board

phial – small glass vessel; vial

filet – laced pattern over mesh   **fillet** – (v.) debone and slice meat or

fish; (n.) narrow strip or band

NB: Fillet is here pronounced "fi-LAY; when pronounced "FIL-let," it refers
to a band for holding hair in place. Filé, ("fee-LAY"), with a long "i," is a spice
derived from sassafras leaves used in Creole cooking. It is almost, but not quite,
a homophone for these words.

filter – (v.) purify, strain, sift; remove impurities through filtration; (fig.) clarify,

oft. by distorting meaning; (n.) sifter

or cloth, used to purify a liquid or gas

philter – love potion, charm (arch.)

filum – (anat.) filament   **phylum** – principal classification of

plants and animals, immediately

below kingdom and above class

find – (v.) uncover, locate; (n.) discovery, usu. of great value

fined – assessed a penalty

finish – (v.) complete; be done with; (n.) exterior texture or quality (*matte f.*)

Finnish – of Finland, or its people,

language, culture, etc.

fir – evergreen tree, pine   **fur** – animal hair, pelt; garment of such

pelts (also, furring, thin wood laths

used in construction)

firs – pl. of "fir"   **furs** – pl. of "fur"; coats, stoles, etc.

made of fur

furze – prickly evergreen; whin

fish – (v.) angle for, seek; try to catch fish; (n.) ember of the phylum *Chordata*

phish – probe for data in computers,

online, etc.; intrude into computer files

fisher – fisherman; kingfisher   **fissure** – crack, chasm

fizz – (v.) froth; (n.) aerated bubbles   **phiz** – (abbr. for physiognomy) face,

expression

flack – press agent, publicist; hype   **flak** – criticism; anti-aircraft fire

flacks – pl. of "flack"   **flax** – plant w. fibers used to make linen

flair – aptitude, style   **flare** – (v.) grow in intensity; blaze with

light; spread like a bell, as a dress;

(n.) emergency beacon or signal

flange – projecting rim   **phalange** – military formation

flea – hopping, biting insect; irritant, nagging concern (*f. in one's ear*)

flee – run, escape

flèche – narrow, arrow-shaped spire in Gothic architecture

flesh – meat; muscle, sinew, and soft tissue of an animal; edible portion of some fruit

flecks – spots, marks

flex – tighten (a muscle); bend a joint, stick, bow, or other object

flew – fled; took to the air

flue – chimney

'flu or **flu** – influenza

flier – handbill, small poster

flyer – aviator; one who flies; rapid train, plane, or bus; opportunity, chance, gamble (*take a f. on*)

floc – light, floating lint-ball; fluff

flock – (v.) join together into a similar group; gather or move together; decorate with flocking; (n.) group of sheep, birds, etc.; congregation

flocks – (v., n.) pl. of "flock"

phlox – varieties of garden flowers

floe – iceberg

flow – (v.) course through a channel; (n.) rate of a liquid's movement

florescence – act or period of blooming; period of great achievement

fluorescence – production of light by the action of X-rays or UV rays on a mineral; light produced thereby

flour – ground meal from grains

flower – (v.) bloom, blossom; unfold; (n.) seed-producing part of a plant; elite (*f. of a nation's youth*)

foaled – gave birth (horses)

fold – (v.) overlay by creasing; quit a card game; (n.) crease; field; (fig.) any group with shared mores; congregation

for – (adv., conj.) in favor; in exchange

fore – (adv.) w. "aft," front of a ship; (n.) leading edge; front; (adj.) ahead of; in front of; (interj.) golfers' warning

four – cardinal number following three

forbear – tolerate; abstain from action   **forebear** – ancestor

forego – precede, go before   **forgo** – omit, relinquish; do without

foreword – introduction   **forward** – (adv.) in a chosen direction;
                                                    (adj.) pushy, flirtatious

fort – stronghold   **forte** – great talent; personal ability or
                                                    strength; accomplishment

NB: Meaning "strength" or "area of expertise," *forte* derives from the French "forte" ("strong"). The "e" is silent. See fuller footnote on p. 104.

forth – forward, onward   **fourth** – (n.) one-quarter of a whole;
                                                    (adj.) ordinal position after third

foul – (v.) defile, pollute; in sports, err; (n.) error (sports); (adj.) putrid, offensive;
                                                    disallowed, out of bounds (*f. ball*)

                                                    fowl – bird(s), esp. domesticated, e.g.,
                                                      chickens, geese, ducks, etc.

fraise – ruff; 16th-century collar   **frays** – (v.) unravels, as cloth; weakens;
                                                    (n.) quarrel, brawl; fright (arch.)

                                                    phrase – idiom; series of words used as
                                                    a group (*participial p.*)

franc – old Fr. monetary unit   **frank** – (n.) hot dog; frankfurter; (adj.)
                                                    open, honest, disingenuous

                                                    Frank – member of an early Germanic.
                                                    tribe; later, a person of Gaul (France)

frees – releases, liberates   **freeze** – place on or in ice; chill; decrease
                                                    temperature to solidify a liquid

                                                    frieze – decorative band; bas relief

friar – religious brother   **fryer** – chicken (for cooking)

fuhrer – (Ger.) leader   **furor** – ado; unbridled public anger

G

Gael – one of Gaelic origin   **Gail**, **Gayle** – female name

                                                    gale – storm, hurricane; high wind

gaff – hook; pike   **gaffe** – embarrassing misstatement

gage – security; greengage var. of plum   **gauge** – measure; scale

gait – way of walking; stride   **gate** – hinged door, esp. in a fence

gaiter – legging, spat; overshoe   **gator** – alligator

gall – (v.) embitter, irritate, appall; (n.) bile, rancor; audacity

                Gaul – France (Lat.); Frenchman

gallop – (v.) to go at a great pace; to hurry; (n.) bounding gait, esp. for horses

                Gallup – NM town bordering Arizona

gamble – wager, bet   **gambol** – frolic

gamin/e – urchin; saucy, roguish girl   **gammon** – (v.) deceive; lash to a spar

                on a ship; (n.) cured ham; nonsense,

                baloney; in Backgammon, a wipeout

gaud – trinket, like tinsel   **god** – deity, idol

gays – homosexuals (sl.)   **gaze** – (v.) stare at; (n.) stare, focus

gees – pl. of "gee," Am. sl. for one thousand dollars (from "a grand")

                jeez – (interj.) gee whiz

gel – colloidal substance   **jell** – set, solidify; come together

gelled – set, firm   **gelid** – icy, chilled

genes – chromosomal sets   **jeans** – trousers, usu. of denim

genet – variety of carnivore, related to the civet; its fur

                jennet – female donkey

geste – gesture (Fr., cf *beau geste*); symbolic action; token

                jest – joke

NB: "Geste" properly has a soft French "zh" sound, while "jest" begins with the sound "dj," but most Americans pronounce both words "djest."

gibe – (v., n.) jeer, taunt   **jibe** – agree, accord withth; tack against

                the wind (naut.)

gild – paint or cover w. gold; doll up; add unneeded detail to (*g. the lily*)

              gilled – having gills, as a fish

              guild – professional or craft associaion

gilt – painted or covered w. gold; gilded **guilt** – responsibility; shame

gin – liquor; card game (gin rummy)   **djinn** or **jinn** – genie, magician

gist – core, heart; basis   **jest** – joke

NB: In this pair of not-quite homophones; the short "i" and "e" are similar enough in some American dialects that the words sound alike.

glair – sizing, glazing; raw egg white used for sizing

              glare – (v.) stare threateningly or angrily;

              (n.) overly bright light; (*g. of the sun*)

gnar – snarl, growl   **knar** – knot; knob of bark on a tree

gnaw – chew, masticate; (fig.) consider, wrestle with a problem or dilemma

nah, naw – no (sl.)

gneiss – metamorphic rock

nice – kind, friendly; nuanced, subtle

gnome – mythical creature

Nome – city in Alaska

gnu – Afr. antelope; wildebeest

knew – was aware of; understood; was acquainted with (a person); had facts at one's command

new – fresh, unused; original

nu – Greek letter "n"; Yiddish expression equivalent to "so?"

Nhu – Madame Nhu, unofficial first lady of Vietnam, 1955-63

goaled – scored a goal

gold – precious metal; yellow hue; (fig.) top award (*g. medal*)

Gobi – desert in Mongolia

goby – predatory tropical fish

gofer – errand-runner; assistant

gopher – burrowing rodent

Google – Am. corporation known for data-search capabilities, cloud storage, and other cutting-edge technology

googol – 10^{100}; numeral one followed by 100 zeros

gored – pierced, as with a rhino horn

gourd – any of several types of fruit growing on vines; cucumber, melon, squash, etc.; dried, hollow shell of such fruit; (fig.) mind (*out of one's g.*)

gorilla – one of the great apes

guerrilla – militiaman; irregular soldier

NB: In Spanish, "guerrilla" is pronounced "ghe-RE-ya" but is usually spoken in English as "grr-IL-uh," similar but not quite identical to "gor-IL-uh."

grade – quality (*G. A*); education level (*seventh g.*); slope, incline

grayed – turned gray; aged (also *greyed*)

graft – (v.) transplant; attach tissue from one body to another; attach shoots of one plant to another; (n.) result of such a process (*skin g.*); political corruption, of which bribery is often part; venality; illicit profit and its results

graphed – plotted on an axis or diagram

grate – (v.) grind by rubbing; irritate, sound harsh; (n.) metal frame or screen

          great – memorable, exceptional

gray – (v.) to age; (n.) mix of black and white; horse defined by color (*an old g.*); (adj.) indeterminate (*many shades of g.*); colorless, drab

          grey – alt. sp. of "gray," esp. horses

grays – (v.) ages; grizzles; (n.) shades, tones, intensities of color; (fig.) subtleties, nuances

          graze – eat grasses, etc. in fields; sample foods, as at a buffet table (sl.)

grease – (v.) ease; lubricate; (n.) oily lubricant; rendered animal fat

          Greece – Mediterranean nation

greave – section of armor, usu. the part covering the shin

          grieve – mourn, regret

grew – enlarged, matured   **grue** – (n.) shiver, as in fear (Scot.)

grill – (v.) broil over hot coals; question relentlessly; (n.) cooking appliance using charcoal, gas, or wood; grilled food

          grille – open grate over a window; decorative bars protecting a car radiator

grip – (v.) grasp, hold tightly; (n.) grasp; small suitcase

          grippe – influenza

grisly – ghastly, horrible   **grizzly** – (n.) genus of bear, *Ursus arctos*; (adj.) grizzled, gray

          (gristly) – full of gristle; tough, chewy

groan – moan, complain   **grown** – adult, mature

grocer – purveyor of foods, groceries   **grosser** – (n.) profitable film (*high g.*); (adj.) fatter; more repellent

---

Numerous words in English have alternate spellings that have the same meaning and are both correct, even if one is more common or "preferred" than the other. Choosing between alternate spellings like "gray" and "grey," or "toward" and "towards," is generally a writer's prerogative, though when a periodical has an editorial preference, the publication's style manual should be followed.

British spellings often differ from American: "cheque" v. "check," "flavour" v. "flavor". For directional words, the British keep, and Americans tend to omit, the final "s": "toward," "upward," "backward," and so forth. Whatever your preference, it's essential to stay consistent within your essay, thesis, novel, etc.

groin – crotch; point of separation of two branches, as of a tree

        groyne – jetty; sea barrier

guessed – estimated   **guest** – visitor

guide – (v.) lead, show the way; navigate; (n.) one who directs or leads a group;

        guyed – steadied; guided as w. a rope

guise – disguise; semblance   **guys** – men, boys; friends; (fig.) team

gunnel – family of northern ocean fish   **gunwale** – upper edge of a ship's side

gym – gymnasium, arena   **Jim** – male name, dim. of "James"

gyve – fetter, shackle (obs.)   **jive** – (v.) speak insincerely; (n.) such

        talk; style of swing music; (adj.) fake

H

hail – (v.) greet, call out to; (n.) frozen rain; onslaught

        hale – healthy, strong

hair – cilia growing from skin or hide on mammals; follicles

        hare – mammal (family *Leporidae*) akin
        to rabbits

hall – passageway, corridor; room   **haul** – (v.) carry, esp. heavy loads; (n.)
        loot, gains (usu. illicit)

halve – cut in half; bisect   **have** – own, hold, possess

Handel – George Frederick, German-born Eng. composer of choral and
        religious music (1685-1759)

        handle – (v.) use, touch, manipulate; (n.)
        doorknob, gripped part of a tool;
        understanding (*get a h. on*)

handmade – crafted without machinery **handmaid** – female servant; a
        subordinate at one's beck and call

handsome – good-looking; attractive   **hansom** – taxicab; type of carriage

hangar – building for storing or repairing airplanes

        hanger – device for hanging clothes; w.
        "cliff-," unresolved ending

hardy – strong, tough; resilient   **hearty** – wholesome, sincere; of good
        heart; rich, filling (*h. stew*)

hardly – scarcely, barely; to a very limited extent

        heartily – warmly, sincerely

haring – scurrying; running away   **herring** – small food fish

hart – male deer; stag   **heart** – blood-pumping organ; center;
                                           core, essence (*the h. of the matter*)

haughty – vain, proud; arrogant, disdainful, usu. offensively so

                                           hottie – sexy, desirable person (sl.)

haute – high, elevated (Fr.) (*h. cuisine*)   **oat** – cereal grass; edible grain

hauteur – haughtiness; disdain (Fr.)   **auteur** – creator, writer; artist; visionary
                                           film writer/director

hawks – (v.) sells, esp. in bazaars, fairs, etc.; (n.) birds of prey; politically, those
                                           who call for confrontation, war, etc.,
                                           rather than negotiation or détente

                                           hocks – (v.) pawns; (n.) varieties of
                                           sweet white wines; parts of a horse's
                                           leg corresponding to the ankles

hay – grass or grain, cut for fodder   **hey** – (exclam.) casual expression of
                                           greeting; hello

Hayes – family name, 19th US president (*Rutherford Birchard H.*)

                                           hays – varieties of grasses or grains
                                           used for animal fodder

                                           Hays – early censor of Hollywood
                                           films (*H. Office*)

                                           haze – blur, mist, fog

                                           heys – (exclam.) casual greetings; hellos

he – masc. pronoun   **hee** – expression of amusement (*tee-h.*)
                                           or derision (*h. haw*)

heal – cure, mend   **heel** – (v.) follow closely; (exclam.) stop,
                                           stay (used to command dogs); (n.)
                                           part of a foot, shoe, or sock; (fig.)
                                           low, base person

                                           he'll – (contr.) he will

healer – physician, nurse; one who heals or comforts; therapist

                                           heeler – in politics, w. "ward," one
                                           who enforces party control

hear – (v.) listen; understand; (interj.) exclamation of support (*"Hear, hear!"*)

                                           here – in this place

heard – listened, understood; sensed

herd – (v.) cause to move together in a group; force together (*h. cats*); (n.) livestock (*h. of sheep*); community with shared characteristics (*h. immunity*) or acting in concert (*h. behavior*)

he'd – (contr.) he would, had, did

heed – obey, listen

heigh – word of greeting, surprise

heed – pay attention; obey

he'd – (contr.) he would, had, or did

hi – (exclam.) word of greeting; hello

hie – hurry

high – lofty; at a high altitude; raised, elevated; (fig.) elated; drunk; under the influence of drugs

heroin – powerful, addictive narcotic derived from morphine

heroine – woman or girl of character or great achievements; central, sympathetic female character in fiction (*romantic h.*)

Hertz – measure of electrical power

hurts – (v.) harms, injures, maims; causes pain or distress (physical or emotional); diminishes; (n.) pains; injured feelings

hew – cut, cut down (trees); obey rules, conform (*h. to a party line*)

hue – color, tint

hic – sound of a hiccough; thus (Lat.)

hick – rustic; unsophisticated person

hide – (v.) conceal, secrete; (n.) skin; pelt, usu. for tanning

hied – hurried, rushed

higher – loftier, at greater altitude; more elated; under the influence of drugs or stimulants to a greater degree

hire – engage, as an employee

him – (pron.) objective form of "he"

hymn – religious song; paean; anthem

hissed – made a sound like a snake; showed dislike, as for a poor performance or villainous character

hist – (interj.) ejaculation meaning "pay attention," "be quiet"; psst

ho – (exclam.) word of greeting; sound of laughter; (n.) prostitute (sl.)

hoe – garden tool used for digging

hoar – frost; rime

hoard – stash; collection

whore – prostitute

horde – vast number, armed host (*the Golden H.*)

whored – prostituted oneself

hoarse – vocally harsh, rasping

horse – (v.) provide a mount for a soldier; (n.) domesticated mammal, genus *Equus*; (fig.) soldiers (*how many h.?*)

hoes – pl. of "hoe"

hose – (v.) direct water through a hose (*h. down*); (n.) flexible tubing used to spray or direct liquid, as from a tap, hydrant, etc.; (n. pl.) stockings

hold – (v.) grip, grasp; wait; (w. "back") temper, restrain; (n.) grip (wrestling); storage space in a boat or plane

holed – (w. "up") hid, went into or stayed in hiding; scored (golf)

hole – opening; passage

holey – full of holes

whole – entire, complete

holy – sacred; revered

wholly – completely, entirely

hollo – (interj.) shout or greeting; hello

hollow – (v.) remove the center of an object (*h. out*); (n.) empty space, hole, cavity, valley, glen; (adj.) empty, void; without effect; meaningless (*h. gesture*)

holm – small island on a lake or river

home – (v.) aim at, direct toward; (n.) house, abode, domicile; in baseball, batter's position (*h. plate*)

hoo – (v., n.) sound of an owl

hooed – p. tense of "hoo"

hoos – p.l. of "hoo"

who – (indef. pron.) what or which person

who'd – (contr.) who would, who had

who's – (contr.) who is

whose – (poss. pron.) belonging to what person

Horace – Roman poet

hostel – inn, boarding house

hostels – pl. of "hostel"

Horus – Egyptian god

hostile – antagonistic, warlike

hostiles – enemy forces

hour – measure of time equaling 60 minutes; appointed time

our – belonging to us jointly

house – (v.) provide housing for   **how's** – (contr.) how is (*h. it goin'?*)

humerus – long upper arm bone in primates, connected to the elbow

                                              humorous – amusing, funny

Hungary – nation in central Europe   **hungry** – in need of nourishment; (fig.)
                                              eager; avid; desperate (*h. for success*)

hurdle – barrier; obstacle   **hurtle** – rush forward; throw, hurl

I

I – (pron.) first person singular   **aye** – yes; a vote in favor

                                              eye – (v.) view with interest; ogle; (n.)
                                              organ of sight; discernment; center
                                              of a storm

idle – passive, unused   **idol** – god, object of worship

ileum – end of the small intestine   **ilium** – part of the pelvis

                                              Illium – (L.) Troy, an ancient city in w.
                                              Turkey, near Gallipoli

immanent – living, inherent; of the divine, present, real (opp. of transcendent)

                            imminent – approaching, anticipated,
                            usu. w. excitement or fear (*i. danger*)

impatience – eagerness; annoyance at delay; anxiety

                            impatiens – genus of flowered plants
                            incl. jewelweed, snapweed, etc.

in – contained by, within, inside; (fig.) popular, currently sought-after (*i. crowd*)

                            inn – hostelry, hotel; restaurant

incidence – act or degree of influence or effect

                            incidents – occurrences, episodes

incite – urge; impel   **insight** – understanding; compassion;
                                  psychological grasp

incompetence – lack of ability; failure **incompetents** – those without talent;
                                             screw-ups

indict – charge with a crime; accuse   **indite** – compose; put in writing

indigence – poverty   **indigents** – poor people; those in need

indiscreet – immodest; blurting out, as secrets; blabbing

                            indiscrete – inseparable; jumbled
                            together in a mass

ingest – eat; take in for nourishment   **in jest** – in a spirit of humor

innocence – purity; naiveté; lack of guilt or responsibility

> **innocents** – those without knowledge; the pure at heart; (fig.) children

ins – (n., pl.) those holding office, elected officials; w. "outs," techniques of an operation or organization

> **inns** – hostelries, hotels

instance – example   **instants** – moments, seconds; very brief passages of time

insurgence – uprising, revolution; alt. sp. of insurgency

> **insurgents** – anti-establishmentarians; opponents of the existing leaders, as of a party

intense – focused, strong, powerful   **intents** – aims, purposes; meanings

intercession – mediation, pleading on someone's behalf; prayer

> **intersession** – short period between regular sessions of a college year

intransigence – stubbornness; refusal to compromise

> **intransigents** – stubborn ones, holdouts; those unwilling to cede or compromise

invade – infringe or encroach upon; attack and enter enemy territory; throng

> **inveighed** – protested, railed against

isle – small island   **aisle** – passage in a church or store

> **I'll** – (contr.) I will

its – third-person possessive pronoun; of or pertaining to something

> **it's** – (contr.) it is

J

jam – (v.) block; improvise (music); (n.) blockage; predicament; fruit preserves

> **jamb** – footer, support (door jamb)

jeans – see *genes*

jewel – gem; precious stone; extremely valued person

> **joule** – unit of energy

jibe – see *gibe*

jo – sweetheart (Scot.)

jo or joe – coffee (sl.)

joe – guy, fellow (*a regular j*.); coffee (sl.)

Juan – Sp. name, equiv. to John

wan – pale, colorless; ill in appearance

Juneau – city, capital of Alaska

Juno – Greek goddess, wife of Jupiter

junkie – addict, user of narcotics, esp. heroin

junky – cheap, lousy; useless

K

kernel – see *colonel*

key – see *cay*

knap – (v.) snap; (n.) summit

nap – short sleep; texture, depth, or character (of hair, carpet)

knar – bark-covered knot

gnar – snarl, growl

knave – rogue; jack (cards)

nave – central part of a cathedral

knead – massage, work; edit

need – (v.) require; must have; lack; (n.) requirement; absence

knew – was aware of; understood; was acquainted with (a person)

gnu – Afr. antelope; wildebeest

new – fresh, unused; original

Nhu – Madame Nhu, unofficial first lady of Vietnam 1955-63

nu – Greek letter "n"; Yiddish expression equivalent to "so?"

knight – soldier; chess piece

night – opp. of day; hours without sunlight; condition of darkness

knit – with needles, make fabric of yarn; furrow (*k. one's brows*)

nit – egg of a louse; idiot ("nitwit"); particular; minuscule error

knob – handle; protrusion

nob – high-born person (sl., ch. Br.); in Cribbage, the jack of the suit drawn

knock – (v.) strike; rap at a door; ram, collide; roam (*k. about*); quit (*k. off*); dismiss, criticize; (n.) rap, punch (*k. on the head*)

nock – (v., n.) notch in an arrow that sets it against the bowstring

knot – looped, tied fastening in thread, rope, cord, etc.; protrusion on a tree; stiffness of a muscle; ache

                                     not – expression of negation

                                     (naught) – nothing; absence of any

knotty – tangled, difficult   **naughty** – bad, misbehaving

know – be aware of, understand; have empirical certainty of

                                     no – (adv.) not in any degree; (adj.) not one, not any (*of n. interest*); (interj., exclam.) opp. of yes; (n.) denial, refusal; negative vote

                                   Noh – form of Japanese drama using masks, dance, and song

know-how – knowledge; ability; talent   **nohow** – (irreg.) in no way; regardless

knows – third-person s. of *know*   **noes, nos** – pl. of "no"

                                     nose – (v.) discover by perseverance (*n. out*); (n.) organ of smell; ability to distinguish scents; taste (*n. for quality*)

L

lac – resinous substance   **lack** – (v.) need, want; have none of; (n.) absence; shortage

                                     lakh – 100,000 rupees; any large sum

lacks – needs   **lakhs** – pl. of "lakh"

                                     lax – easygoing; flexible, non-rigid

lade – load; ladle out   **laid** – p. tense & p. part. of "lay"; set down, placed; w. "out," arrayed, displayed; for fowl, deposited an egg

lager – light beer   **logger** – tree-cutter; one who harvests trees as a crop

lain – p. part. of "lie"; had reclined, become prone or supine (*had l. in bed*)

                                     lane – path; road; traffic guideline

lair – den, hideout   **layer** – stratum, tier; coat; producing hen

      NB: These are homophones primarily in the southern U.S.

lam – flight; run, escape   **lamb** – young sheep, or its meat; (fig.) naif, innocent; gentle person

lama – Tibetan priest, monk   **llama** – Andean ruminant of the camel
family (ch. Peruvian) (in Spanish,
pronounced "ya´-ma")

lap – seat created by a person sitting; (fig.) embrace, cradle (*l. of luxury*)

Lapp – of or pertaining to Lapland

laps – pl. of "lap"   **lapse** – (v.) backslide; err; (n.) slip,
error; pause; break, hiatus

lay – (v.) place, set; (w. "out") arrange; p. tense of "lie" as in "recline"; (n.)
contour (*l. of the land*)

lei – floral necklace of Hawaii

les – the (Fr. pl.; e.g., *Les Miz*)

lays – pl. of *lay*   **leis** – pl. of *lei*

laze – (v.) idle, loll, do nothing; (n.)
haze of hydrochloric acid, minuscule
glass particles, and toxic gases
formed when lava meets seawater

lea – meadow, field; measure of yarn   **lee** – (n.) shelter sheltered place, away
from the wind; (adj.) sheltered, out
of the wind

leach – filter, ooze through   **leech** – bloodsucking worm, valued for
anti-coagulants in medical treatment;
physician (obs.); (fig.) dependent,
hanger-on

lead – (n.) dense, malleable element; (adj.) referring to objects of lead (*l. pipe*)

led – (v.) went first; showed the way;
conducted (an orchestra); (n.) light-
emitting-diode (L.E.D.)

NB: The element "lead" (noun, rhymes with "bed") and the verb "to lead"
(rhymes with "feed") are homonyms, not homophones, spelled but not pronounced the same. The past tense of "to lead" is "led" without an "a."

lead – (v.) go first, precede; conduct, oversee, take charge; (n.) most active part;
starring role; clue, hint, suggestion;
leash, harness; (adj.) most important

lede – start of a story (journalism)

lied – Ger. song, oft. romantic or sad

leader – chief, director; head person; guide; one who goes first

           liter or **litre** – metric unit of volume

leaf – part of a plant; page   **lief** – (adj.) beloved (obs.); (adv.) gladly; willingly (arch.)

leak – (v.) escape accidentally (fluid); seep out; secretly disclose; (n.) hole, crack; unauthorized disclosure

           leek – tart, edible bulb, genus *Allium*

lean – (v.) rest on or against; tilt; (adj.) slim; without fat

           lien – mortgage; property claim

leant – leaned, tilted; tended toward   **lent** – made a loan

           Lent – traditional Christian period of fasting before Easter

Lear – Shakespearean king; brand of jet   **leer** – ogle, stare lustfully

leas – meadows, fields   **lees** – dregs, residue from wine

leased – rented   **least** – smallest amount

lends – gives temporarily, oft. w. security   **lens** – optical glass ground for focus and magnification in glasses, telescopes, etc.

lessen – abate, diminish   **lesson** – something learned; insight

lesser – minor; less important   **lessor** – holder of a lease; landlord; one who rents out property

lets – allows, permits; rents, leases out   **let's** – (contr.) let us

levee – dam, breakwater; early evening reception (ch. Br.)

           levy – (v.) impose (a fine); (n.) tax, impost

liable – obligated for damage, at fault; tending to (do, suffer); likely, apt

           libel – (v.) defame in print; (n.) false, malicious, derogatory statement

NB: Libel is defamation in print; slander refers to malicious speech.

liar – dishonest person   **lyre** – ancient stringed instrument

lichen – "dual" plant comprising a fungus and an alga in symbiosis

           liken – compare

licker – one who licks   **liquor** – alcoholic beverage; extract or distillation of a grain or flower

           likker – liquor (sl.)

           (potlikker) – liquid remaining from cooking greens (collard, mustard, etc.)

lie – (v.) speak falsely; be found; recline, be at rest; (n.) falsehood, misstatement; position (golf); terrain (Br.*)*

        lye – alkaline solution, oft. used in soap and other cleansers

lieu – place; stead   **loo** – bathroom (ch. Brit.)

lightening – easing of a burden; removing darkness (*a l. sky*)

        lightning – electric discharge in a storm; high speed (*as fast as l.*)

limb – branch of a tree; arm or leg   **limn** – portray; describe

links – parts of a chain; connections, bonds; a golf course

        lynx – large, short-tailed wildcat

literal – word for word; sans interpretation; unvarnished (*l. truth*)

        littoral – intertidal; of the seacoast

lo – (interj.) expression of awe, discovery, or unveiling; voilà (*l. and behold*); (adj.) low (sl., ch. advertising) (*lo-cal*)

        low – (v.) make a soft sound (cattle); (n.) atmospheric condition of low pressure; (fig.) state of depression; (adj.) not high; sad; unworthy; disgraceful

load – (v.) put onto a carrier; fill up; burden; (n.) burden, onus; weight

        lode – vein of ore (*mother l.*); trove, discovery; source for research, etc.

        lowed – mooed, as cattle

loan – (v.) lend; (n.) act of lending; something borrowed or lent; mortgage

        lone – only, single, solitary

loath – unwilling, hesitant   **loathe** – hate, abhor, detest

locale – site, area, region   **lo-cal** or **low-cal** – dietetic, nonfat

lochs – inlets, lakes, deep bays, ch. in Scotland and Scandinavia

        locks – (v.) fastens with a key; shuts; (n.) hasps, bolts; tresses, hair

        lox – smoked salmon (Ger., Yiddish)

Loki – minor god of Norse mythology   **low-key** – understated, restrained

loon – bird known for its mournful cry; (fig.) crazy person; idiot

        lune – crescent-shaped mark on the surface of a sphere; leash for a hawk

loop – (v.) entwine, twist; flip in midair; (n.) circle, esp. in a rope; noose; circuit of a plane on a horiz. axis (*l. the l.*)

loupe – eyeglass used by jewelers

loos – toilets (Br.)

lose – misplace; go down to defeat; be bested by an opponent

loot – (v.) pillage; denude; steal; (n.) stolen goods

lute – medieval stringed instrument similar to a guitar

lore – folk wisdom; tales

lower – (v.) bring down; opp. of raise; (adj.) not as high; beneath (*l. berth*)

lucks – w. "out," has good fortune

luxe – luxuriant; posh, expensive

lumbar – of the lower back

lumber – (v.) tread heavily, plod; (n.) wood milled and planed for use

M

ma – (dim., colloq.) mother

maa – sound made by a sheep

maw – mouth, jaws; grip of any powerful machinery or institution

mac – (n.) term of address for a male; (exclam.) pal, buddy; mister; mackintosh

mack – mackintosh (ch. Brit., colloq.)

madder – (n.) genus of plants, esp. used in dyeing; crimson color; (adj.) comp. of "mad"; angrier; more emotionally unstable, crazier

(matter) – (v.) count, signify; (n.) substance, material; subject; value

made – constructed, built

maid – housekeeper; damsel, virgin, unmarried woman (arch.)

mail – (v.) send by postal service; (n.) any item thus transported

male – masculine; opp. of female

main – (n.) large pipe for distributing water; (adj.) primary; first among equals

Maine – northeastern-most Amer. state

mane – on a horse or lion, the hair on the neck; any thick tresses

maize – corn

maze – series of paths leading to a hidden center; confusing pattern

mall – shopping center   **maul** – tear up; batter with claws

                                                              moll – prostitute; gangster's girl

mandrel or **mandril** – machining spindle or rod

                                                              mandrill – primate known for blue and
                                                              scarlet markings on its face and rump

manikin – dwarf; anatomical model of a human, often used in medical training

                                                              mannequin – model of a human body
                                                              used for fitting or displaying clothing;
                                                              woman who models clothing

manner – style, method; sort, ilk   **manor** – palace, estate; (fig.) high birth
                                                              (*to the m. born*)

mantel – shelf atop a fireplace; ledge   **mantle** – (v., n.) cover; cloak

mark – (v.) highlight, incise; signify; (n.) trace, impression; indicator, sign; stain,
                                                              stigma (*m. of Cain*); illiterate person's
                                                              signature; former Ger. currency

                                                              marque – emblem, symbol, logo

marks – (v.) identifies; writes on; signifies; (n.) pl. of "mark"

                                                              Marx – German-Jewish family name

marquee – theater sign   **marquis** – Br. and Fr. rank of nobility

marquees – pl. of "marquee"   **marquise** – wife or widow of a marquis;
                                                              elongated, pointed oval cut (58 facets)
                                                              of a gemstone; ring with such a stone

marry – wed; combine, join together   **Mary** – female name; traditionally, the
                                                              mother of Jesus

                                                              merry – gleeful, foolishly happy

marshal – (v.) gather; organize, esp. military forces; (n.) officer; sheriff, deputy

                                                              martial – military; related to warfare
                                                              and battle (*m. arts*)

marten – carnivorous, tree-dwelling mammal w. valuable fur

                                                              martin – bird of the swallow family

mask – (v.) conceal; hide; disguise; (n.) face covering used for disguise or protection

                                                              masque – costumed entertainment

massed – gathered, marshalled; placed together for power or effect

                                                              mast – pole holding sails (nautical);
                                                              fodder for bears, wild boars, etc.

mat – small rug; padded mattress for wrestling, yoga, etc.

matte – (v.) offset artwork behind glass w. thick mounting paper; (n) such paper; (adj.) dull, nonreflective (*m. finish*)

me – first-person objective pronoun

mi – traditional third note of the musical scale (*do, re, mi...*)

mead – alcoholic beverage brewed from fermented honey; meadow

Mede – one of a mid-Eastern people, ancient rulers of Persia

mealie – corn (S. Afr.)

mealy – dry, powdery; tasteless

mean – (v.) signify, denote; intend; (n.) median, average; norm; (adj.) unkind; shabby, poor; despicable

mien – bearing; posture; attitude

meat – edible flesh of animals or birds; (fig.) key part; gist, substance

meet – (v.) encounter; be introduced to; (n.) contest; (adj.) appropriate, fitting

mete – (v.) dole out, apportion; (n.) boundary line

medal – (v.) win, place; gain a prize; (n.) award, oft. worn on the chest;

meddle – interfere inappropriately, usu. without invitation or appreciation

(metal) – element or alloy displaying certain chemical properties

meddler – one who meddles; busybody, yenta

medlar – shrub of the rose family; its fruit, used in jelly, etc.

meow – sound made by a cat

miaou – alt. sp. of "meow" (ch. It.)

mere – (n.) pool, pond, small lake; (adj.) minor, of little importance

Mir – space station launched by the Soviet Union, now defunct

mescaline – alkaline drug, extracted from the peyote cactus; peyote

mesclun – salad mix of greens

metal – malleable element or alloy displaying certain chemical properties

mettle – strength under pressure; will, willpower; determination

mewl – cry, whine

mule – sterile offspring of a donkey and horse; beast of burden; (sl.) drug courier

mews – (v.) cries, as a kitten; (n.) walkway; alley, small street

muse – (v.) ponder, consider; (n.) any of nine Greek goddesses believed to inspire art (music, dance, theater, poetry, etc.) and wisdom

mic – microphone (sl.)

mike – (v.) amplify sound using a microphone; (n.) alt. sp. of "mic"

mica – translucent mineral; isinglass

Micah – male name; biblical prophet

micks – the Irish (sl., derogatory)

mix – (v.) stir, blend together; (n.) mixture, combination; variety

middy – loose blouse or shirt with a sailor collar; midshipman (sl.)

midi – skirt or dress reaching between the knee and the mid-calf

might – (v.) could; may; possibly will or can; (n.) power, strength

mite – nit; tiny parasite

mil – measure of thickness

mill – (v.) fabricate, esp. tools; grind grain or metal; (n.) factory for grinding; kitchen implement (*pepper m.*)

mild – gentle, soft; not intense

miled – ran miles in a race

mince – (v.) chop finely; (n.) chopped meat, mincemeat

mints – (v.) coins money; establishes its value; (n.) facilities for coining money; government agencies in charge of such activity; aromatic plants of the genus *Mentha*, used in cuisine and medicine; flavors derived from them, e.g. spearmint, peppermint, etc.; candies using such flavors

mind – (v.) watch over; care; tend (*m. your manners*); (n.) brain, intelligence; concern (*keep in m.*)

mined – extracted from the ground, as ore, minerals, etc.; drawn from the sea; made use of (data)

miner – worker in a mine

minor – (n.) child; underage person; (adj.) of little import; lesser (*Asia m.*); diminished, in musical keys

minion – servant; medium type size; typeface designed for Adobe systems

minyan – quorum of ten Jews needed for worship in a synagogue

mink – mammal w. valuable fur; such pelts used in coats, stoles, etc.

minke – type of whale w. valuable oil

minks – pl. of "mink"

minkes – pl. of "minke"

minx – flirt; saucy girl; seductress

missal – book of sequential Catholic texts for use through a year

missile – weaponized part of a rocket used in warfare; any projectile used as weaponry

missed – failed to meet; regretted; pined for; shot wide, away from a target

mist – haze, fog

moan – make a sound of discomfort; experss forlorn fear; (fig.) complain, agonize, whine (*m. and groan*)

mown – cut or shorn, as a lawn or hay

moat – water-filled trench protecting a castle, town, etc.

mote – speck; irritating object

mode – style; type; sort

mowed – (p. tense of "mow") cut grass, silage, etc.; w. "down," killed, as by a vehicle or firearms

model – (v.) shape, form; display, as clothing; (n.) ideal, paragon, mentor; small simulacrum (*m. car*); mannequin; (adj.) ideal; representational (*m. home*)

mottle – spot; mark with spots

modeled – (v.) shaped; displayed; wore (as a mannequin)

mottled – spotted, unevenly colored

moil – drudgery; labor

moyel – Jewish official who circumsises boys shortly after birth

moiré – patterned in waves; of fabric, metal, or metallic paper so patterned

moray – aggressive carnivorous eel, oft. found in coral reefs

molding – (v.) shaping, forming by hand (clay, etc.); turning rotten; (n.) cornice, contoured, sometimes elaborate, edging, oft. just below the ceiling

moulding – alt. sp. of "molding"

moo – (v., n.) sound made by a cow   **moue** – pout; grimace

mood – temperament; atmosphere (of a group); emotional state (*in a foul m.*)

mooed – made the sound common to cattle; lowed

moose – largest member of the deer family, weighing up to 1,500 lbs.

mousse – fluffy, egg-based food; hair-setting gel

moral – (n.) lesson; ethical precept (usu. pl.); (adj.) ethical, good

morel – gourmet mushroom

morays – pl. of "moray" (see *moiré*, p. 55)   **mores** – customs, ethos

mordant – (n.) substance for fixing dyes in fabrics; corrosive used to etch lines, designs, etc.; (adj.) sarcastic, caustic

mordent – ornamentation in music

morn – dawn; early daytime   **mourn** – grieve

morning – first half of the day; hours between midnight and noon

mourning – (v.) grieving; (n.) formal period of grief; clothing worn to indicate sorrow or loss

morro – small hill   **morrow** – morning; tomorrow

mucous – (adj.) containing mucus   **mucus** – (n.) lubricating secretion of the mucous membranes

murderess – female murderer   **murderous** – lethal; willing to commit murder; extremely angry (*in a m. rage*)

murre – genus of diving shorebirds   **myrrh** – gum resin used in incense

muscat – sweet wine grape   **musket** – longbarrel rifle

muscle – (v.) w. "in," intrude; (n.) sinew; strength; enforcer (sl.)

mussel – bivalve mollusk

(muzzle) – (v.) gag, silence, censor; cover a dog's or horse's mouth to prohibit biting; (n.) front of an animal's face; front end of a rifle

mussed – tousled, messy

must – (v.) have to; be required to; (n.) obligation; mould (of wine)

mustard – herb used in cooking; when processed, tart dressing for food

mustered – gathered (troops)

N

Nader – Ralph, Am. author/activist

nadir – rock bottom, lowest point

nae – see *nay*

nap – see *knap*

naught – none, zero

knot – (v.) tie rope, string, etc.; (n.) result of such tying; woodgrain showing location of a branch

not – (adv.) negative; the opposite

naughty – bad, misbehaving

knotty – tangled, difficult

naval – of ships, or a navy

navel – umbilicus; bellybutton; navel orange

nave – central part of a church building

knave – rogue; jack (in cards)

nay – no; negative (as a vote)

nae – no; none (Scot.)

née – born (Fr., fem.), indicating a married woman's birth name

neigh – (v.) whinny; (n.) the cry of a horse

neap – of lower, less extreme ocean tides; opp. of spring tide

neep – turnip (Br.)

need – (v.) require; must have; lack; (n.) requirement; absence

knead – massage, work; (fig.) edit text

neum or neume – sign in medieval church music designating certain notes

pneum – combining form of "pneuma," referring to breathing, lungs, etc.

new – fresh, unused; original

gnu – African antelope; wildebeest

knew – was aware of; understood; had sexual relations w. (bibl.)

Nhu – Madame Nhu, unofficial first lady of Vietnam 1955-63

nu – Greek letter "n"; Yiddish expression equivalent to "so?"

nice – kind, friendly; nuanced   **gneiss** – metamorphic rock

nicks – cuts slightly; steals (ch. Br.)   **nix** – (v.) put a stop to; (adv.) negative; no

night – darkness; opp. of day; (fig.) despair, utter lack of hope

knight – (arch.) mounted soldier; hero,
swain (*k. in shining armor*); chess piece

nit – egg of a louse; w. "-wit," simpleton   **knit** – using needles, make fabric of
yarn; furrow (*k. one's brows*)

no – see *know*

nock – see *knock*

Nome – city in Alaska   **gnome** – mythical creature; sprite

none – zero; absence; (fig.) person of no religious affiliation

nun – woman in a religious order; (fig.)
prude, puritan

O

oar – paddle for rowing boats   **or** – alternatively

ore – metal-bearing rock

ode – poem, usu. of praise   **owed** – (v.) p. tense of "owe"; (adj., p.
part.) payable; due (of a debt)

offed – murdered, killed (sl.)   **oft** – often

oh – expression of surprise   **owe** – be in debt; have an obligation
(see p. 4 for more homophones for
"oh," including "au," "aux," and "eau")

olé – bravo, esp. for bullfighters (Sp.)   **au lait** – w. milk (*café a.*) (Fr.)

oleo – margarine   **olio** – miscellany; mixed collection;
olive oil (It.)

one – (n.) smallest cardinal number; (adv.) single; only, solitary

won – took the prize, was victorious;
earned an award

opal – gemstone; female name   **Opel** – French-German automobile

ordinance – law; rule   **ordnance** – ammunition; firepower

ought – should; is obligated to   **aught** – any; some; zero (usu. for a
year, e.g., *nineteen a. two* [1902])

oui – see *we*

our – see *hour*

overate – ate too much; sated oneself   **overrate** – value too highly

overdo – exaggerate; go too far; cook too long, burn (food)

overdue – late (as in payment of a debt or the arrival of a train, etc.)

overseas – abroad   **oversees** – supervises

P

pa – (dim., colloq.) father

pah – exclamation of disgust, disbelief

paw – (v.) manhandle; (n.) foot of a dog, cat, etc.; hoof

PAC – political action committee

pack – (v.) stow (in luggage); tamp down; carry (a gun); (n.) knapsack; group of dogs or hyenas; Cub Scout group; informal club (*the "Rat P."*)

paced – walked back and forth

paste – (v.) fasten with adhesive; (n.) glue, adhesive; (adj.) false, esp. of gemstones

packed – (v.) stowed, put away, as a suitcase, trunk, or storage area; carried in a knapsack, etc.; (adj.) tightly fitted; tamped down

pact – treaty, agreement

packs – (v.) stows, as a suitcase; carries (*p. a gun*); (n., pl.) knapsacks

Pax – peace (Lat., cf *P. Romana*)

paddy – flooded basin or terraced pond for growing rice

patty – ground meat, packed into shape for frying or grilling

NB: Unlike many "d" and "t" words, the pronunciation of these words and their derivatives – in which the doubled letter follows a stressed syllable – is almost identical in American English.

paid – gave what is due; retired a debt; made worthwhile, profited (*p. off*)

payed – alt. sp. of "paid" (obs. except w. "out"); let out slowly, as rope or cable

pail – bucket

pale – (n.) (fig.) limit, boundary; region of acceptable behavior (*beyond the p.*); (adj.) colorless, ashen

pain – (v.) discomfort, sadden, distress; (n.) hurt, ache; (fig.) irritant (*p. in the neck*)

      pane – flat piece, usu. of glass; framed section of a window

pair – set of two; duo; dyad

      pare – peel, cut away rind or excess; remove layers

      pear – variety of fruit akin to apples

palate – part of the mouth receptive to flavor; sense of taste

      palette – range of color; board used by an artist for holding paints

      pallet – platform, usu. for shipping

pall – (v.) become boring, tiresome; bore; satiate; (n.) covering for a coffin; (fig. or lit.) miasma; shadow, gloom

      pawl – pivoted bar allowing a notched wheel or ratchet to rotate in only one direction

Pampas – a region of Argentina

      pampas – a type of wild grass

      pompous – self-important, egotistical

pan – (v.) sieve to discover or separate precious ores or metals (*p. for gold*); in the arts, review negatively, dismiss; rotate a film camera laterally; (n.) flat cook-cookware for frying; shallow basin; natural depression in the earth; leaf of the betel plant; chewable substance derived therefrom

      panne – soft, velvety fabric; feather (Fr.)

par – average (*p. for the course*)

      parr – young salmon

parity – equality; balance

      parody – satire; humorous takeoff, often warm-hearted

parlay – (v.) turn gambling winnings into a larger bet; (n.) accumulation of bets

      parley – conference between opposing sides in a battle

(**parodying**) – poking fun at, usu. with mimicry or satire

      (**parroting**) – repeating by rote; aping

passed – succeeded at (a test); exceeded, outdid; overtook

      past – ago, no longer applicable

patience – endurance; forbearance; at cards, the game of solitaire (Br.)

patients – medical clients

pauper – one who is poor

popper – basket for popping corn; amyl nitrate, a drug used to treat heart disease; inhalant used for euphoria or to induce sexual excitement (sl.)

pause – (v.) wait; halt; (n.) brief stop; hesitation; surprise (*give one p.*)

paws – (v.) mauls, manhandles; (n.) front and rear feet of mammals (other than apes and monkeys)

pea – edible seed, contained in a pod

pee – urinate (sl.)

peace – calm; harmony; absence of war

piece – part of a whole; musical or artistic composition

peak – apex; mountaintop

peek – (v.) espy, look at sneakily; (n.) brief glance, often illicit

pique – (v.) spark, as interest; intrigue; (n.) snit; fit of irritation

peal – chime, ring (a bell)

peel – (v.) strip; pare; remove a layer; (n.) rind, skin

pearl – nacre; semi-precious gem from an oyster shell; valuable insight (*p. of wisdom*)

purl – knit a reverse stitch; make loops with cord or twine

pedal – (v.) propel by using pedals; (n.) foot control lever used to propel bicycles, control looms, sewing machines, etc.

peddle – retail; sell, trad. on the street

petal – showy part of a flower

peer – (v.) gaze, stare; study, look closely at; (n.) equal (*jury of one's peers*); one with a title; noble (ch. Br.)

pier – dock; jetty; structural column

pekoe – type of tea of India and China

picot – looped edging on lace

pelisse – long cloak, of or lined w. fur

police – (v.) patrol, oversee; maintain order; (n.) uniformed force, quasi-military, that maintains order and obedience to law or regulations; (adj.) pertaining to such a force or action

penal – of or relating to punishment; punitive, corrective

penile – of or relating to the penis

pencel – small pennant

pencil – implement for writing, usu. of wood w. graphite

pendant – something hanging, such as an ornament from a necklace

pendent – hanging; undecided, pending

penitence – regret; atonement

penitents – those asking forgiveness

penned – wrote; held captive, corralled

pend – hang, dangle; await (action)

per – for; apiece; from, via, by way of

purr – (v., n.) sound made by a cat

perc – percolate; bubble up; develop

perk – (v.) w. "up," become alert, pay attention; (n.) perquisite; side benefit

permanence – stability; unchangeability

permanents – chemical hair treatments used to induce long-lasting curls

perse – dark blue (Persian blue)

Perse – nickname for Persephone or Persis (ch. Br.)

purse – (v.) pout; press (lips) together and outward to express disapproval; (n.) pocketbook; container for coins

pervade – invade, disperse throughout

purveyed – provisioned; furnished food to a gathering, troops, etc.

phase – stage in a cycle

faze – surprise; knock off balance

phial – small glass vessel; vial

file – (v.) sort, organize, place with other like items; (n.) folder to hold papers; cabinet for such folders; rasp

phlox – see *flocks*

phosphorous – (adj.) containing or related to phosphorus

phosphorus – (n.) element #15

pi – ratio of the diameter of a circle to its area (3.14592535 ad infinitum)

pie – any food baked in a crust, filled w. vegetables, meat, fruit, etc.; pizza; diagram of that shape (*p. chart*)

pic – (abbr.). picture, photograph (sl.)

pick – (v.) opt, choose; harvest (n.) choice; best option (*p. of the litter*)

pica – 12-point type; abnormal food craving, as for clay or dirt

pika – family of lagomorphs, kin to hares

picked – (v.) chose, opted for, selected; (adj., p. participle) harvested, as from a fruit tree, shrub, etc. (*fresh-p. tomatoes*)

Pict – one of an ancient British people

pidgin – patois, dialect

pigeon – type of dove; girl (sl., ch. Br.); dupe; spy; (w. "stool") tattler, rat

Pilate – title of the Roman procurator of Judea (*Pontius P.*)

pilot – (v.) guide, steer (as a plane or ship); (n.) conductor, navigator; (n., adj.) first in a series (*TV p.*)

pile-on – (n.) collective pressure

pylon – upright tower carrying power lines, etc.; structure supporting an airplane engine, fuel tank, etc.

pistil – female, seed-bearing organ of a flowering plant

pistol – short-handled gun; (fig.) doer, activist, dynamic person

pix – pl. of "pic"

picks – chooses, elects; votes for

pixelated – divided (an image) into pixels, as for digital display

pixilated – confused; drunk; in Celtic myth, led astray by pixies

place – (v.) put; locate; (fig.) remember (*I can't p. her*) (n.) location; social status (*know one's p.*)

plaice – food fish (ch. Br.)

plain – (n.) steppe; extensive treeless fields; prairie; (adj.) unadorned

plane – (v.) smooth; shave rough edges (usu. of wood); (n.) airplane

plait – (v., n.) braid, weave

plate – platter, serving dish; silverware, utensils, urns, etc.; dental insert

plantar – of the sole of the foot

planter – one who plants; plantation owner (obs.); decorative container holding flowers, shrubs, etc.

pleas – admissions (legal) (*copped a p.*); requests, demands

please – (v.) satisfy, elate; (interj.) word of request, oft. used w. humility

pleural – of or pertaining to the membrane covering the lungs

plural – more than one; multiple, many

plots – (v.) schemes; plans; draws outline for; (n.) sections of land set aside for a building, grave, etc.; shemes, plans (usu. illicit); storylines, narratives (in plays or operas, etc.)

    plotz – collapse w. emotion (Yiddish)

plough – tool used to make furrows; alt. sp. of "plow" (ch. Br.)

    plow – (v.) furrow; dig through (a book or chore); (n.) plough (Am. sp.)

plum – fruit-bearing tree; its fruit; sloe **plumb** – (adj.) straight, true; vertical (*p. line*); (adv.) completely, utterly (sl., ch. southern Am.) (*"He's p. crazy."*)

pocks – pustules, as in smallpox; scarring marks left by such pustules

    pox – any disease symptomized by skin eruptions (*chickenp.* or *smallp.*); (fig.) plague, curse (*a p. on both your houses*)

pokey – jail, prison (sl.)   **poky** – slow, dilatory

polar – of or relating to the N. or S. pole; (fig.) utterly different (*p. opposites*)

    poler – one who poles a boat or raft

pole – (v.) push and steer a boat; (n.) long, cylindrical stick; northern or southern axial end of the earth

    poll – (v.) survey a population's opinions; trim, shave (a sheep); (n.) opinion survey; voting place; election results

politic – rational, wise, prudent; unscrupulous; expedient

    politick – engage in politics; run for office; campaign

poof – (interj.) sound signifying disappearance; (n.) disparaging term for a gay man (sl., ch. Br.)

    pouffe – hassock, usu. tufted; footstool

populace – citizenry, residents; whole number of a region's people

    populous – densely inhabited

pore – (v.) read thoroughly; study, analyze; (n.) opening in the skin

    pour – discharge a liquid or powder from a container; rain heavily; use unsparingly (*p. it on*)

Porsche – Italian automobile brand; family for whom it is named

                                     Portia – female name

praise – (v.) laud, honor, worship; express respect; (n.) acclaim; worship

                                     prays – addresses the divine; seeks guidance, favor, forgiveness, etc.

                                     preys – attacks, victimizes (w. "on")

pray – ask of, esp. a deity; hope   **prey** – (v.) attack, victimize (w. "on"); (n.) animal hunted for food; victim of a sniper, con artist, etc.

precedence – greater importance, higher status; order of entry in formal affairs or diplomacy

                                     precedents – prior court rulings; justifications; examples

precedent – previous ruling; example, justification

                                     president – presiding officer of an organization, business, nation, etc.

prefix – syllable before a word to change its meaning (e.g., *dis+ease=disease*); word used as an honorific

                                     prix fixe – set price (Fr.); on menus, cost of a comprehensive meal

premier – (n.) chief or prim minister under some parliamentary systems of government; (adj.) highest, best

                                     premiere – debut; first public showing

presence – company (of); surroundings; appearance, arrival

                                     presents – gifts, donations

pride – ego; self-satisfaction; hauteur, arrogance; family of lions

                                     pried – snooped, spied; forced open

pries – snoops, spies; asks unwelcome questions; forces open

                                     prise – force open, oft. w. a lever

                                     prize – winnings; award, honors

primer – beginner's lesson book   **primmer** – more prim or prudish

prince – royal ruler; son of royalty; heir apparent; ideal; nice guy (*You're a p.!*)

                                     prints – (v.) writes w. noncursive letters; (n.) copies of pictures or photos; smudge marks; fingerprints

principal – (n.) head of a school, college, etc.; business owner or officer; amount of a loan; (adj.) main, primary

principle – philosophical tenet; ethical basis; rationale

profit – (v.) gain; (fig.) learn from; (n.) return on investment; value

prophet – seer, religious visionary

pros – professionals; reasons for support **prose** – plain, nonpoetic writing

psalter – biblical book of Psalms **salter** – one who salts or preserves meat

psammite – sandstone (obs.) **samite** – expensive medieval cloth, often woven w. gold or silver threads

psammon – microorganisms found in waterlogged sand, as on a shore

salmon – (n.) food fish of the family *Salmonidae*; (n., adj.) pinkish-yellow color similar to the flesh of such fish

psych – (v.) (w. "out") manipulate; (n.) (abbr.) psychiatry, psychology; (adj.) psychiatric, psychological

cyc – (abbr.) cyclorama; translucent curtain used in stage sets

pupal – of or pertaining to the pupa stage of insect development

pupil – student; part of the eye through which light is focused onto the retina

purest – most pure or unadulterated **purist** – one upholding rigid standards; absolutist

NB: This is another pair of not-quite homophones, but close enough to sound identical in some contexts.

puttee – cloth wrapped to cover the lower leg, like a gaiter

putty – soft, malleable mixture or chalk and oil, to secure and waterproof window panes, tiles, etc.

putts – final strokes in golf; tap-ins **putz** – penis (Yiddish); jerk, idiot (sl.)

Q

quail – (v.) cower in fear; quiver, shake; (n.) game bird; partridge

Quayle – family name; Dan, U.S. vice-president (1989-92)

quarts – quarters of a gallon; U.S. and Br. liquid measure

quartz – crystalline mineral used in scientific applications, jewelry, etc.

quay – see *cay*

NB: In American English "quay" can be pronounced "kay" or "key."

quean – brazen woman, hussy (obs.)   **queen** – female ruler of a kingdom; powerful, accomplished woman (*Aretha Franklin, q. of soul*); high-ranking playing card or chess piece; gay male, oft. used to designate effeminacy (sl.)

quince – thorny decorative shrub; its tart fruit, used for baking (*q. pie*)

quints – (abbr.) quintuplets

R

rabbet – (v.) to cut wood so as to form a joint; (n.) section cut from wood to allow another piece to fit tightly together

rabbit – (v.) hunt rabbits; w. "on," prattle, chatter (Brit.); (n.) rodent akin to hares; fur of the animal

race – (v.) hurry, rush; vie against in a contest of speed; (n.) competition, in sports; political contest; fast course of water; any of the primary human population groups, as distinguished by genetic traits or their manifestations

res – thing, in law; matter (*r. publica*)

rack – (v.) arrange; amass (*r. up points*); struggle to remember (*r. one's brain*); (n.) shelving unit; framing (*clothes r.*); mechanical lift; baked ribs (*r. of lamb*); medieval torture device; havoc (*r. and ruin*); antlers; bosom (sl.)

wrack – (v.) disturb violently, convulse; (n.) ruin; wreckage

racket – noise; dishonest scheme; scam; flat, stringed bat for tennis, etc.

racquet – alt. sp. of "racket" (ch. Br.)

radical – (n.) in Mathematics, number derived from a root; in politics, extremist;
advocate of fundamental, structural
change; (adj.) pertaining to the root
or elemental structure; fundamental;
extreme; concerning the root number
radicle – root part of a seedling; rootlet;
start of a nerve or anatomical structure

raid – (v.) invade; attack; make a sneak visit (*r. the refrigerator*); (n.) invasion, foray
rayed – spoked; emanating from a
center point

raiding – invading, attacking   **rating** – (v.) assigning a value to; (n.)
measure, value; assessment

rain – (v.) pour down; teem (*r. cats and dogs*) (n.) water droplets from clouds
reign – rule, governance; realm
rein – (v.) hold back; slow (w. "in"); (n.)
leash for controlling animals

raise – (v.) lift; pose (a question); improve (*r. spirits*); grow livestock, produce, or
(colloq.) children; increase a bet; incite
(*r. Cain*); (n.) increase (pay, bid, wager)
rays – beams; radii; flat fish with
winglike fins (*manta r.*)
raze – level, tear down to the ground

raki – alcoholic beverage popular in Greece, Albania, Turkey, Iran, etc.
rocky – full of rocks, uneven; unsteady

rancor – bitterness; long-lasting spite; malice (Br. sp. "rancour")
ranker – (n.) enlisted man; (adj.) more
vigorous; coarser, more offensive;
growing more wildly; smellier

rap – (v.) hit sharply (*r. one's knuckles*); perform rap music; (n.) style of spoken
music; gossip, reputation; record of
arrests (*r. sheet*)
wrap – (v.) cover, sheathe; bring to an
end (*w. up*); (n.) covering, scarf, shawl,
etc.; type of stuffed tortilla sandwich;
protective cover or material (*plastic w.*)

rapped – p. tense of "rap"

rapt – enchanted, enraptured; intense (*r. attention*)

wrapped – p. tense of "wrap"

rapper – one who raps; rap musician

wrapper – shawl, mantle; protective cover

ray – beam; directed light

re – traditional second note of the musical scale (*do, re, me*)

read – perused, scanned

red – (n.) one of six primary colors on the spectrum seen by the human eye; anger (*see r.*); (adj.) of that color; self-conscious, blushing (*r. as a beet*)

read – (v.) peruse, scan; interpret words on a page; (fig.) understand (*I r. you*); analyze, figure out, make sense of (*r. the signs*) (n.) book, story (*a good r.*)

rede – counsel, sage advice (obs.)

reed – stem of a plant; ancient writing implement made from such a plant

Reade, Reed, Reid – variations of Br. and Am. surnames

NB: These variant spellings reflect national origins (Scotland, Ireland, England). Cognates include "rede" (counsel), indicating a person in the position of counselor or advisor. King Ethelred's sobriquet "the Unready" [sic] meant he was ill-advised, or did not heed good advice.

real – true; substantial; factual, provable by empirical means

reel – (v.) stumble, be stunned; pull w. a winch (*r. in*); (n.) device for reeling in fish (*rod and r.*); traditional folk dance, line dance (*Virginia r.*)

reave – steal, rob; take by force

reeve – (v.) fasten w. rope through a ring; (n.) chief officer, bailiff; fem. sandpipers (irreg. pl. of "ruff"

rec – abbr. for "recreation"

reck – reckon, consider (arch.)

wreck – (v.) ruin, destroy; smash up; (n.) smash-up, accident; car in terrible condition; haggard person; someone in dire straits

recede – ebb, flow back; retreat   **reseed** – sow again, as grass

NB: These two words differ slightly in stress: "recede" carries clear emphasis on the second syllable, while both syllables of "reseed" are equally empasized.

receipt – record of payment; recipe (obs.)   **reseat** – install again, as in office; reelect

recite – declaim, by rote, lines, poetry, etc.   **resite** – relocate; place at a different site

reek – (v., n.) smell, stink   **wreak** – cause, bring about (*w. havoc*);
                                              render, effect

reference – citation; acknowledgment; connection; thing or citation referred
                                              to; resource, as a dictionary

                                    referents – things or people referred to

referral – recommendation; citation   **refurl** – roll up again, as a flag or sail

relaid – reinstalled, as tile, stones, etc.   **relayed** – sent; forwarded, passed on,
                                              as a message

Reo – former American manufacturer of motor vehicles, 1905-75

                                    Rio – Rio de Janiero, city in Brazil known
                                              for Carnival; (Sp.) river (*R. Grande*)

residence – home, domicile   **residents** – inhabitants; citizens

rest – (v.) relax; take a break; sleep; (n.) respite; relaxation; break from work;
                                              musical symbol indicating a pause

                                    wrest – take by force

retch – vomit; choke   **wretch** – miserable person, loser

review – (v.) examine, inspect; analyze; critique; (n.) examination; critique of a
                                              play, book, film, etc.

                                    revue – variety show, usu. w. music

Rex – masc. name; king (Lat.)   **wrecks** – (v.) destroys, smashes; (n.)
                                              ruins; hulks; broken remains

rhea – large, flightless bird of S. Am.   **ria** – long, narrow inlet; river mouth

rheum – post-nasal drip; cold   **room** – (v.) reside at, as a boarding
                                              house; (n.) part of a building defined
                                              by walls, door, etc.; sufficient space
                                              for comfort (*elbow r.*); scope (*r. for doubt*)

rheumy – afflicted by rheum; runny-nosed; sniffling

                                    roomie – roommate (sl.)

                                    roomy – spacious, comfortable

                                    Rumi – 10th c. Persian-language poet

rho – Gr. letter (see *roe*)

Rhodes – Gr. island; Cecil, Br. imperialist, philanthropist (R. *scholarship*)

> **roads** – streets, lanes; (fig.) routes,
> pathways (*all r. lead to Rome*)

rhyme – poetic scheme using similar sounds; meter; rhythm; (fig.) sense, logic
> (*without r. or reason*)
> **rime** – frost, frozen dew

rick – (v.) pile hay; (n.) stack of hay, etc. in a field, before baling
> **wrick** – strain, wrench

riffed – played music ad lib, or as thematic background for a soloist
> **rift** – fissure; break, separation due to
> disagreement

rigger – one who rigs, as sails, etc.   **rigor** – firmness, strictness; the stiffness
> of death (*r. mortis*)

right – (v.) straighten, align; correct; avenge, atone for (*r. a wrong*); (n.) ownership,
> legal interest; that which is equitable,
> just, or fair; (adj.) correct, true; fair;
> (fig.) politically conservative,
> reactionary (*r.-wing*)
> **rite** – formal ceremony; ritual;
> accomplishment (*r. of passage*)
> **write** – form letters and words; be
> literate (*read and w.*); originate a
> story, play, poem, novel, etc.;
> correspond with (*w. to friends*)
> **Wright** – family name, ch. Br. and Am.
> **-wright** – craftsman, repairman

NB: The spelling "-wright" is used most frequently in compound forms: cart-wright, playwright, shipwright, wheelwright, etc. Because of the wide range of such skills, family names with a prefix (Cartwright, Wainright) are fairly common, as is the name "Wright."

"Right" derives from Old English "riht," and before that Indo-European "reg" meaning straight. "Rite" comes from Latin "ritus" and before that the Indo-European "rei," from a word meaning join, or fit. A few millennia later, both are pronounced the same in modern English.

ring – (v.) peal, toll, as a bell; (with "up") call by phone (ch. Br.); (w. "in") surround; celebrate (*r. in the new year*); (n.) torus; circular shape, object, dance, etc. (*r. around the rosie*); jewelry, usu. for ears or a finger (*signet r.*); group, usu. criminal (*smuggling r.*)

wring – squeeze; dry out

rise – (v.) go higher, waft in the air; get out of bed; achieve higher status (*r. in the world*); (n.) hill, upward slope; promotion; raise in pay (ch. Br.); reaction, oft. negative (*g. a rise out of*)

ryes – pl. of "rye"

ritz – elevated style; ornateness, attitude of self-conscious fancy (*put on the r.*) elegant hotel chain (Ritz-Carlton)

writs – legal decrees; orders

road – street, lane, pathway; (fig.) route, way (*r. to ruin*)

rode – p. tense of "ride"; made use of a vehicle or animal for transport

rowed – p. tense of "row"

roc – mythical giant bird

rock (v.) move back and forth in rolling, repetitive motion (*r. the cradle*); make unsteady (*r. the boat*); exude hipness; be fashionable; (n.) stone of various sorts (granite, basalt, etc.); (fig.) large gem; (fig.) anything solid, reliable

roe – fish eggs; caviar

rho – 17th letter of the Gr. alphabet

row – (v.) use oars to propel a boat; (n.) tier; line, segment

roil – stir up, muddy

royal – pertaining to royalty; regal

role – function, use; part in a play

roll – (v.) turn over; toss; flatten (as with a rolling pin); rob; (n.) baked bun; ongoing success (*on a r.*); sound of drums, esp. ceremonial

rondeau – stylized poem of 15 lines

rondo – movement in a musical composition, usu. a sonata

'roo – kangaroo (ch. Austr.)

roux – cooked mixture of butter and flour, used as a base for sauces

rue – (v.) regret; (n.) herb, shrub

rood – cross, crucifix

rude – impolite, boorish; unfinished

rued – regretted

roomer – renter, boarder

rumor – tale, unsubstantiated story

root – (v.) propagate by rooting; dig; seek, nose out; (w. "out") weed; discover and remove; (n.) part of a plant that draws nutrition from soil; underlying cause; origin

route – (v.) send via; forward; (n.) path, direction (see also *rout*)

rose – (v.) ascended; surfaced; awoke, got out of bed; stood (n.) perennial flowering plant, family *Rosaceae*, or its flower; hue of such flowers; (adj.) pale pink

rows – (v.) uses oars; (n.) tiers, levels

rot – (v.) decay, spoil; degenerate; (fig.) go bad, become corrupt; (n.) putrefaction; destructive aspect, often hidden

wrought – p. tense of "wreak"; created, formed, worked as by a craftsperson (*w. iron*); brought about, caused

rote – memorization; repetition

wrote – p. tense of "write"

rough – (v.) attack (*r. up*); live without amenities (*r. it*); (n.) in golf, unmown, weedy area (adj.) uneven; not refined; approximate (*make a r. guess*); difficult

ruff – (v.) in Bridge, to trump; (n) the act of ruffing; stiff collar (arch.); on some animals, a decorative collar of feathers, fur, or skin

rouse – awaken; stir up

rows – arguments, disputes; fights

rout – (v.) overcome (foes); expel; (n.) thorough, utter loss; disaster

route – (v.) send via; (n.) path, road, direction (see also *root*)

rude – impolite; coarse, vulgar; rough, unrefined (*a r. dwelling*)

rued – regretted, wished undone

rues – regrets; feels sorrow for   **'roos** – pl. of "'roo"

                                          ruse – scheme, plan

rung – p. participle of ring; telephoned (ch. Br.); (n.) crossbar on a ladder; step

                                          wrung – squeezed dry; spent

rye – wheatgrass; liquor   **wry** – sardonic; ironic; dryly sarcastic

S

sac – pouch, usu. filled w. fluid   **sack** – (v.) put in a bag; fire, dismiss (sl.);

                                          (n.) bag (*s. lunch*); dry sherry

sachet – scented bag   **sashay** – strut, prance; walk in an

                                          exaggeratedly feminine manner

sacks – pl. of "sack"   **sax** – saxophone

sail – (v.) move by wind power, as a boat or kite; leave, depart; accomplish with

                                          ease; (n.) heavy canvas cloth

                                          sale – exchange of payment for wares

                                          or services (*for s.*); discount (*on s.*)

sake – Japanese fermented rice liquor   **Saki** – Br. writer, H. H. Munro

salver – tray, usu. for presenting cards, papers, food, etc.

                                          salvor – salvager, as of ships or cargo

sane – sensible, rational   **seine** – (v., n.) net, sieve, filter

                                          Seine – river in France

NB: "Sane" is pronounced with a long "a," as is "seine"; while English-speakers generally pronounce the river the same way, "Seine" in French is spoken as "sen."

sari – traditional draped and wrapped garment of India, usu. of silk

                                          sorry – regretful, sad; pathetic

saurel – horse mackerel; lizard   **sorrel** – (n.) bitter, edible weed of the

                                          buckwheat family; (adj.) reddish-brown

saver – one who saves   **savor** – (v.) taste, smell, esp. w. delight;

                                          (n.) flavor, aroma

scalar – of measurement by scales   **scaler** – one who climbs or ascends

scene – part of a play; stage set; setting; in painting, a landscape; unruly public

                                          behavior (*make a s.*)

                                          seen – p. participle of "see"; noticed,

                                          observed

scent – aroma; trace, hint   **cent** – U.S. coin worth 1/100 of a dollar

                                                  sent – dispatched; mailed

scull – (v.) to row with sculls; (n.) long, narrow racing boat, or its oar

                                                  skull – the skeletal head

'scuse – contr. for excuse (*'s. me*)   **skews** – twists; distorts

sea – ocean; vast quantity   **see** – notice, observe; view

                                                  See – diocese; administrative district,

                                                      esp. Catholic (*Holy S.*)

sealing – see *ceiling*

seam – line or border, esp. of sewn fabric; joint; layer (*s. of coal*)

                                                  seem – appear, pretend

seaman – sailor   **seamen** – sailors

                                                  semen – fluid containing sperm

sear – scorch, burn on the surface; harden, make callous; wither

                                                  seer – prognosticator; prophet

                                                  sere – arid, dried up; withered

seas – oceans; vast amounts   **sees** – observes, notices

                                                  seize – take by force; grasp; make use

                                                      of an opportunity (*s. the day*)

secs – moments, instants (sl.) (*a few s.*); dry wines

                                                  (**sects**) – religious subgroups; cults

                                                  sex – gender, esp. in animals; (fig., sl.)

                                                      intercourse

seed – see *cede*

seeder – see *cedar*

seek – search for; chase   **Sikh** – of or pertaining to an Indian

                                                      religion; member of that religion

                                                      (also pronounced "sick")

segue – seamless transition   **Segway®** – one-axled, two-wheeled,

                                                      gyroscopic self-propelled scooter

seller – see *cellar*

senate – parliamentary body   **sennet** – ceremonial trumpet call in

                                                      Elizabethan drama

                                                  sennit – fabric made of braided rope or

                                                      yarn; plaited grass used in making hats

senser, sensor – see *censer, censor*

seraph – angel of the highest order

serif – in typesetting, a fine stroke that projects from the main stem of a letter

serf – peasant; indentured worker

surf* – (v.) ride waves on a surfboard; visit Internet sites (*s. the web*); (n.) swell of the ocean near shore

serge – twilled woolen fabric

surge – (v.) swell quickly; (n.) wave, swell (water); a sudden increase

serious – solemn; sincere

Sirius – a binary star; the "Dog Star"

session – meeting, scheduled period

cession – formal ceding of rights

sew – stitch; weave together

so – thus; to such an extent

sow – plant; (fig.) inculcate (*s. hatred*)

sewer – one who sews; seamstress, sempster, tailor

sower – one who plants, scatters seeds

NB: "Sewer" (SO-ur) in the above meaning is also a homonym (word spelled the same) for "sewer" (SOO-ur), a liquid waste disposal system.

shake – (v.) agitate, stir; tremble; (n.) milkshake; thick flavored mixture of milk, ice cream, etc.

sheik – Arab ruler of a tribe or clan; elder; noble; learned man

NB: Most Americans pronounce "sheik" as if it rhymes with "chic"; however, the traditional pronunciation, reflecting the transliteration of the Arabic word, rhymes more closely with "shake" or, in some dialects, "shah-EEK."

shanty – hovel; poor dwelling

chantey – rhythmic sailor's song

shear – cut hair; poll, remove fleece from sheep, goats, alpacas, etc.

sheer – steep, precipitate; unrestrained (*s. unmitigated gall*); thin, translucent

shears – clippers; pruners

sheers – translucent window drapes

shier – (n.) horse that shies; (adj.) alt. sp. of shyer

shire – county, administrative area (Br.)

shyer – more modest

---

* English adopts new words and meanings more easily than some other tongues. "Surf" originally meant just a line of breaking ocean waves; it morphed into a verb describing the sport of surf-boarding; and that usage led to "surf the web,": to skip across the surface for pleasure before being drawn in ... or under.

shirr – cook eggs in a container, usu. in boiling water; make a type of ruffed
gathering in fabric

sure – (adj.) certain, confident; (adv.)
indeed; "yes," used as an answer

NB: "Shirr" is properly pronounced with a schwa (sh*ʌr*), "sure" with a longer
"o" sound (sh*oor*). But in casual speech they are often identical.

shoe – (v.) put steel protectors on a horse's feet; do a farrier's job; (n.) footwear;
horseshoe

shoo – (exclam.) command to pets or
pests (cf, *Scram! Get out!*)

shone – shined; gleamed; (fig.) stood out   **shown** – p. participle of "show"; proven,
demonstrated; modeled, presented

shoot – (v.) discharge (an arrow, bullet, etc.); (fig.) command to speak (*I'm ready:
s.!*); (n.) young emerging plant stem

chute – passage; slide; (abbr.) parachute

shudders – shakes; shivers   **shutters** – hinged, often folding panels
used to protect windows

sibilance – hissing sound   **sibilants** – consonants like "c," "s," or
"z" that create sibilant sounds

sic – thus (Lat.); like this, this way (in print, used to indicate an original error)

sick – ill; perverted

Sikh – a member of a monotheistic,
egalitarian Hindu religion (also
pronounced to rhyme w. "seek")

sic 'em – (exclam.) attack   **Sikkim** – state in the Himalayan
highlands of India

sics – sets upon; sends after, as a dog   **six** – cardinal number after five

side – lateral surface, part; half; team   **sighed** – p. tense of "sigh"

sighs – exhales heavily, w. a sound of regret or contentment

size – dimension; mass; scope

sight – view; visual range   **cite** – refer to; name

site – location

Advertising generates neologisms along with linguistic corruption. "Light"
becomes "lite" and "right" "rite" (Rite-Aid). Avoid confusing "cite," "site," and
"sight" with this mnemonic: "A good realtor will cite the sight-lines of the site."

sign – (v.) append a signature; (w. "off") approve; (n.) omen; indication

                                sine – a ratio in trigonometry

signet – seal, official mark   **cygnet** – young swan

silence – absence of sound; (fig.) unwillingness to talk; keeping of secrets

                            silents – early silent films

sin tax – levy on disapproved behavior, e.g., gambling, alcohol

                                syntax – grammar; the structure, use,

                                and meaning of language

sink – (v.) fall; diminish; lose altitude; (n.) bowl for drainage (*kitchen s.*); low area

                        where water gathers

                        sync – agreement; (abbr..) synchronicity

Sioux – Am. Indian nation   **sou** – old French coin

                        sue – bring legal action against

slay – kill; (fig.) amuse deeply   **sleigh** – sled, designed to slide on snow

                        using runners, usu. drawn by horses;

                        bed styled to resemble a sleigh

sleight – dexterity, skill; cunning; manipulation; fakery (*s. of hand*)

                        slight – (v.) treat with disdain; ignore;

                        (n.) insult; rude dismissal; (adj.) minor,

                        of little consequence

slew – (v.) killed, slayed, usu. in war; (n.) vast number; sudden spate

                        slough* – (pron. "sloo") bog, marsh, fen

                        slue – pivot; turn; swivel

sloe – blackthorn; wild plum   **slow** – (v.) retard; diminish speed; (adj.)

                        at low speed; unintelligent

slough* – (pron. "sluff") (v.) shed, cast off; gloss over; elide (in speech); (n.)

                        castoff layer; dead tissue; on a snake,

                        outer layer of skin that is shed

                        sluff – (v., n.) discard at cards, esp. Bridge

*NB: "Slough" when pronounced to rhyme with "now" means "backwater"; a state of moral degradation or spiritual dejection, as in *the slough of despond*. "Slough" can also be pronounced "sloo" in its meaning of "backwater."

Crossword puzzles, British acrostics, and word-based board games such as Scrabble®, Pictionary®, etc., can improve your word knowledge. But to win, you still need to know how to spell the word you want to use—or its homophone!

snees – knives, daggers (arch.)

sneeze – (v.) expel breath explosively, in reaction to irritation, congestion, etc.; (fig.) express respect for (*nothing to s. at*); (n.) such an act

soak – (v.) wet thoroughly; saturate; (n.) sot, drunkard (sl.)

soke – (arch., Br.) jurisdiction of a court

soar – take win; fly; sail high in air; succeed beyond expectations

sore – angry; irritated; (w. "at") carrying a grudge; aching, in pain

soared – p. tense of "soar"

sword – long-bladed steel weapon; saber, scimitar

sol – trad. fifth note of the musical scale (*do, re, mi, fa, s.*)

sole –(v.) furnish with a bottom (*s. a shoe*) (n.) type of flatfish; its filet; bottom of a shoe, sock, or foot; (adj.) lone, single, solitary

soul – spirit; heart; essence

Seoul – capital city of S. Korea

sold – exchanged for money; convinced

soled – attached soles to shoes

some – indefinite quantity; a few, any

sum – (v.) total; add up; (n.) total

son – male offspring

sun – Earth's star

sorceress – female magician; witch

sorcerous – having to do with sorcery

sot – tippler; alcoholic

sought – looked for, searched for

sough – (v.) make a sighing sound, as of wind in trees; (n.) such a sound

sow – female pig or bear

spade – shovel; one of a suit of cards; offensive term for an African American, now obsolete

spayed – neutered (female animals)

spec – estimate, speculation (*on s.*)

speck – mote, iota, tiny amount

speiss – metallic mixture from smelting

spice – (v.) add spices to foods; (fig.) add excitement (w. "up"); (n.) one of many extracts from plants, used in cooking to add flavor

spits – expectorates; speaks venomously

spitz – one of several varieties of dogs, incl. Pomeranian, Samoyed, etc..

'stache – moustache (sl., ch. Amer.)   **stash** – (v.) hide, conceal; store; keep for
                                            emergencies (as cash); (n.) secret cache
                                            of money, food, drugs, etc.

staff – (v.) hire, fill jobs; (n.) employees; team of military officers; rod used as a
                                            symbol of authority; lines on which
                                            music is notated

                                            staph – staphylococcus virus

staid – stoic, unflappable; stern   **stayed** – remained in place; took up
                                            residency, usu. temporary (*s. overnight*);
                                            paused; held back, restrained

stain – (v.) discolor; leave a visible residue; (fig.) besmirch; blemish; (n.) mark left
                                            on cloth by dirt, grime, etc.; blemish
                                            on one's character or reputation

                                            stane – stone (var., Scot.)

stair – stairway; riser   **stare** – gaze at, ogle

stake – (v.) announce, reserve (*s. a claim*); wager (*s. one's reputation*); (n.) investment;
                                            pointed stick; fencepost; ecclesiastical
                                            division in the Mormon faith

                                            steak – any of numerous cuts of meat,
                                            usu. beef

stalk – (v.) follow, as prey; tail; track; (n.) plant stem

                                            stock – (v.) replenish supplies; carry, as
                                            merchandise; (n.) inventory, supply;
                                            share of a company; liquid extract of
                                            vegetables, meat, poultry, etc., used in
                                            cooking; confidence, faith (*put no s. in*);
                                            estimate, appraisal (*take s. of the situation*);
                                            part of a rifle behind the barrel; (adj.)
                                            basic, unexceptional; repertory or
                                            traveling theater troupe (*summer s.*)

stamen – pollen-producing male reproductive organ in plants

                                            Stayman – Samuel, popularizer of a
                                            bidding convention in Contract Bridge

stationary – unmoving; fixed in place   **stationery** – personalized writing
                                            paper; letterhead

steal – (v.) take without authorization; rob; sneak (*s. away*); (n.) bargain; good deal

    steel – iron alloy; (fig.) determination, will; epitome of strength (*Man of S.*)

    stele – surface, usu. of stone, prepared for engraving

steer – (v.) guide, pilot; navigate; (n.) castrated bull, raised for meat

    stere – cubic meter

step – (v.) move using feet or paws; take action; (n.) pace; action taken, usu. to achieve a greater goal (*first s.*)

    steppe – temperate, treeless plains, esp. in Russia and Argentina

sties – pl. of "sty"

    styes – pl. of "stye"

stile – gate, gated crossing

    style – mode; type; fashion

stolen – robbed, taken illicitly (*s. kiss*)

    stolon – horizontal plant runner that develops roots to propagate

straight – perfectly aligned; uncurved; direct, honest; ethical (*on the s. and narrow*); heterosexual (sl.)

    strait – narrow sea passage

straighten – align; even up

    straiten – constrict, make narrower

strider – one who strides

    stridor – harsh breathing sound from congestion of the lungs, larynx, etc.

sty – pen, esp. for hogs: (fig.) messy room, house, office, etc.

    stye – inflammation of the eyelid

subtler – more nuanced, discreet

    sutler – camp follower (arch.); seller of provisions to soldiers on the march

succor – assist those in need

    sucker – confidence-man's mark; sap, one easily taken in

succulence – savor, deliciousness

    succulents – several plant species with fleshy tissues for storing water

suede – tanned leather

    swayed – bent back and forth, esp. in wind; influenced a decision

suite – rooms; apartment; matched set of furniture, luggage, etc.

    sweet – sugary; nice, innocently kind

summary – recap; precis

    summery – like summer; flowery, warm, balmy

superintendence – supervision; oversight   **superintendents** – overseers; supervisors, of school districts, buildings, etc.

surplice – loose, wide-sleeved ecclesiastical garment; type of dress

surplus – (n., adj.) extra, overage

swat – hit, slap   **swot** – pored; crammed (ch. Br.)

swath – wide strip, as cut by a scythe or mower; (fig.) broad impact

swathe – (v.) swaddle (an infant) in soft cloth; bandage a wound; wrap, as in a sari; (n.) bandage, strip of cloth

sword – see *soared*

symbol – representation; icon, ideal   **cymbal** – percussion instrument of brass, usu. used in pairs

T

tacet – be silent (musical)   **tacit** – unspoken; implied, as approval

tach – (abbr.) tachometer   **tack** – (v.) hammer in; fasten, as with a pushpin; add (*t. on*); sew cloth w. loose, temporary stitches; reset sails to catch wind (naut.); (n.) small brad, nail; gear (equestrian)

tachs – pl. of "tach"   **tacks** – (v.) fastens with a brad; sews cloth w. loose, temporary stitches; shifts course; (n.) short, sharp brads, usu. w. broad heads; small nails

tax – (v.) strain, tire, overuse; (n.) levy, government impost

tacked – p. tense of "tack"   **tact** – polite concern for feelings; sensitive, perceptive speech

tael – Asian unit of weight; equivalent unit of money (arch., Ch.)

tail – (v.) follow; stalk; (n.) external, articulated spinal extension on many animals; posterior, buttocks (sl.); rear part of an airplane; last of a group

tale – story, saga (*A T. of Two Cities*); fable, myth; fib, lie (*tall t.*)

tahr – wild goat of S.E. Asia

tar – (v.) apply oil-based sealant; pave a road, using tar; (fig.) besmirch, disparage (*t. with the same brush*); (n.) sealant made of hydrocarbons, wood, etc.; sailor

taint – (v.) infect, as with poison; stain; make corrupt or useless; (n.) infection; trace of corruption, etc.

'taint – isn't; it ain't (Am. sl.)

tao – Taoism; Chinese philosophy of simplicity and selflessness

tau – Greek letter "t"

NB: Proper pronunciation of "tao" is "dow," but most Americans use the "t" rather than "d" sound.

taper – (v.) decrease in thickness at one end; diminish; w. "off," come to an end; (n.) narrow candle

tapir – long-snouted S. Am. mammal

tare – empty weight of a vehicle or container

tear – (v.) rip, rend; (n.) rip in fabric or paper; streak, binge (*on a t.*)

taro – Asian plant tuber used to make poi

tarot – mystical cards used for fortune-telling

tartar – hard calcium deposit on teeth; extract (*cream of t.*) used in wine, etc.

tartar (sauce) – tangy, mayonnaise-based sauce, usu. served w. fish

Tartar – disciplinarian; strict, bad-tempered person, harridan

tarter – more tart or biting; tangier

taught – instructed, educated

taut – tight, tense

tot – infant, young child; nip, quick drink, esp. of alcohol (ch. Br.)

taupe – dark gray-brown

tope – drink to excess (of alcohol)

tea – aromatic plant; beverage made from its leaves, or any plant; concentrated liquid extract, as from compost

tee – peg used in golf; casual shirt

ti – trad. seventh letter of the musical scale (*do, re mi, fa, sol, la, ti*)

tea time – the hour for a light afternoon meal, usu. 4:00-6:00 p.m. (ch. Br.)

tee time – starting hour for a golf game

team – (v.) join together, w. "up"; (n.) group working together, often in
harness; sporting group or club

teem – abound, swarm

tear – (pronunced "teer") drop of saline fluid moistening the eyes, eyelids, etc.

tier – row of seats in a stadium; layer,
as of a wedding cake

tearable – subject to being torn   **terrible** – awful, ruinous

teas – pl. of "tea"   **tease** – jibe, mock; back-comb (as hair)

'tec – detective (sl.)   **tech** – technician; one with knowledge
of electronics, computing, etc.

tel – arch. mound, hill in the Middle East **tell** – (v.) relate; narrate, as a story;
tattle; (n.) signifier, indicator, usu.
unconscious, as a gambler's habitual
posture, motion, etc.

temped – worked as a non-permanent, short-term employee

tempt – entice; offer, usu. in exchange
for a desired or illicit benefit; seduce;
provoke risk (*t. fate*)

tempera – type of painting using an albumen or colloid (e.g., egg yolk) instead
of oil

tempura – deep-fried, battered seafood
or vegetables

tenner – ten pounds, ten-pound note (Br.) **tenor** – high male voice; singer
in that vocal range; attitude, mood,
tendency; purport; general character

tern – shore bird; sea swallow   **turn** – (v.) rotate; spin; ponder (w.
"over"); shape with a lathe; subvert
(*t. a spy*); (n.) place in a rotation (*take
one's t.*)

ternary – tri-part; in three segments   **turnery** – work of a lathe; lathe shop

terrene – of the earth; worldly   **terrine** – earthenware dish for cooking

tureen – deep, lidded earthenware dish
for soup, stews, etc.

Thai – of, pertaining, or referring to Thailand, its cuisine, culture, etc.; Siamese

(tai) – from "T'ai chi ch'uan," a form of Chinese martial arts

tie – (v.) loop fabric, rope, string, etc. into a knot; fasten objects together using a knot; make even (a score); (fig.) join together, as in marriage (*t. the knot*); (n.) length of fabric used as a bowtie, ascot, etc.; dead heat; (fig.) bond between people, nations, etc.

Tye – the name of rivers in Virginia and Washington state

their – (poss. pron.) belonging to others; relating to a third party

there – (adv.) opp. of "here"; in that place; (interj.) when repeated, words of comfort; (excl.) behold, voilà

they're – (contr.) they are

therefor – in lieu of; for this, that

therefore – thus, as a result; hence

threw – past tense of "throw"; tossed; (fig.) confused, stunned (*t. me for a loop*)

through – by way of; finished, done

throe – spasm or pang, of pain

throw – (v.) toss, hurl; deliberately lose (*t. a game*); (n.) toss, pitch

throes – (n.) pl. of "throe"; struggle, as over a decision, fate, etc. (*death t.*)

throws – pl. of "throw"

throne – seat of power

thrown – p. participle of "throw"

thyme – savory herb

time – duration; period of existence

tic – nervous spasm

tick – (v.) measure time; elapse (*the clock is t.-ing*); (n.) half the sound of a clock (*t.-tock*); usu. infectious blood-sucking insect

---

Possibly the most familiar English-language homophones are "their," "there," and "they're," as all three words are common in everyday conversation. When spoken, context makes it easy to know which is meant, but the written forms trip up even accomplished writers (and typists). In a likely tie for second place are the pairs "who's" and "whose," and "it's" and "its." Maybe it's the apostrophe's fault!

tide – cycle of ocean movements in tandem w. the lunar orbit (fig.) an inexorable historical or cultural change (*t. of history*)

    tied – knotted; fastened with rope, etc.; frustrated (*fit to be t.*)

tighten – close more firmly; tie (a knot) more tightly

    Titan – (n.) mythological giant that first populated the heavens; (fig.) important person (*t. of industry*)

'til – abbrev. for "until"   **till** – cash register; money drawer

to – toward, in the direction of; in one's opinion (*it seems t. me*)

    too – also; overly, excessively

    two – whole number after one

toad – amphibian of the genus *Bufo*, kin to frogs; (fig.) despicable person

    toed – having toes (*three-t. sloth*)

    towed – p. tense of "tow"

tocsin – alarm bell; its sound; any alarm   **toxin** – poisonous substance

toe – (v.) drive with the toe (*t. a football*); hit at an angle (*t. a nail*); obey* (fig.) (n.) digit on the foot or paw

    tow – pull, haul with a rope or chain

toke – (v., n.) inhale/inhalation, usu. on a marijuana cigarette

    toque – hat, usu. brimless

told – narrated, related; tattled; showed the effects of a strenuous effort

    tolled – pealed, as a bell

tole – lacquered metalware   **toll** – (v.) peal, ring; (n.) fee to cross a bridge or road; count, total (*death t.*); burden, consequence (*a heavy t.*)

ton – two thousand pounds; (fig.) a great weight, burden; a lot (*a t. of money*)

    tonne – Br. sp. of "ton"; metric ton weighing 1,000 kilograms

    tun – barrel, cask

---

* Many authorities say "toe the line" (obey) derives from British naval usage: sailors were required to stand for inspection with the toes of their boots at the edge of a plank. Others spell it "tow the line," derived from the tow ropes used to pull barges in a canal, with "line" referring to the rope yoked to teams of horses or oxen. "Toe the line," however, is the more widely accepted standard form.

tongue – muscle in the mouth, used for speech, taste, etc.; language (*native t.*); sass, backtalk, lip; flap of a shoe; spit of land, peninsula

tung – Asian tree; oil from that tree

tool – implement; utensil

tulle – netted fabric for veils, etc.

'toon – cartoon (sl.)

tune – musical composition; air

tor – hill; mountainous crag

tore – made a hole in or ripped fabric; rushed, ran speedily

tort – wrongful act, in law

torte – cake; rich, eggy dessert w. nuts

tough – (n.) hoodlum, gang enforcer; (adj.) difficult; hard, thick; of meat, fruit, vegetables, gristly, fibrous; hard to chew or digest; (interj.) dismissive, unsympathetic comment, meaning "too bad"

tuff – porous, igneous rock

toughed – p. tense of "tough"; endured, w. "it" and "out" (*t. it out*)

tuft – (v.) form tufts in fabric using evenly spaced buttons, ties, etc.; (n.) a clump or gathering of feathers, fabric, etc.

tracked – followed, traced

tract – lot, site; expanse of land; system (*digestive t.*); pamphlet, usu. religious

trader – merchant; broker

traitor – betrayer of a country or cause; one who commits treason

transience – impermanence

transients – travelers, ones passing through; temporary visitors

tray – platter for holding, serving, carrying, esp. food

trey – three, esp. in card games

TripTik – travel map showing routes, esp. popular in 1950s–1980s U.S.

triptych – three-part religious painting

troop – group, throng; body of soldiers, organized group of Boy or Girl Scouts

troupe – group of actors or buskers

trooper – member of a state police force; cavalry soldier

trouper – one who perseveres; reliable person; dutiful performer

trussed – tied up, as a bird for cooking **trust** – (v.) repose confidence in; rely on; (n.) confidence, faith; monopoly; type of financial investment or arrangement of funds for one or more named beneficiaries (*t. fund*)

tucks – (v.) tightens in place; secures, as a shirt into trousers; (n.) gathers or pleats in fabric; basted pleats to tighten garments

tux – abbrev. for tuxedo

turban – wrapped head cover **turbine** – type of engine or power source

twill – woven woolen fabric **'twill** – (contr.) it will

U

ugli – kind of tart fruit; tangelo **ugly** – unattractive; homely; revolting

undo – negate; reverse **undue** – inappropriate; intrusive

unreal – fantastic, supernatural; astonishing; (fig.) remarkable, memorable

unreel – unroll, as a hose or thread

use – utilize; avail **yews** – pl. of "yew"; any of several trees or shrubs of the genus *Taxus*

youse – irreg. pl. of "you" (*y. guys*)

NB: "Youse" can be heard in NY and Boston; parts of Ontario and Nova Scotia.; and parts of England, Scotland, Ireland, Australia, NZ, and S. Africa.

V

Vail – city in Colorado **vale** – valley, glen

veil – diaphanous headcovering; (fig.) shroud, curtain (*v. of secrecy*)

vain – egotistical; proud **vane** – rotating implement used to determine wind direction

vein – blood vessel; seam of ore; mode, subject (*in the same v.*)

valance – short horizontal drape across a window, table, bed, etc.

valence – number given to an element indicating chemical bonding qualities

vaper – person who smokes using an electronic device

vapor – mist, smoke; brief phenomenon; something unsubstantial; gaseous state

vapers – pl. of "vaper"

vapors – pl. of "vapor"; (arch.) nervous condition; hysteria; fainting spell

variance – divergence from existing data; degree of variation; permission to differ from rules or regulatory norms; dispute, quarrel

variants – alternative forms, such as versions of spelling, narrative, etc.

vary – change, alter; exhibit several different aspects

very – extremely; intensively; to a great extent or degree

verses – stanzas in a poem

versus – against; as compared to

vial – narrow tubular container for medicine, etc.; small glass bottle, phial

vile – gross, revolting; base, despicable

W

wack – crazy person (*w. job*)

whack – hit, smack

waddle – (v., n.) walk like a duck, w. short steps, swaying side to side

wattle – material of mud and sticks for building primitive walls, roofs, etc.; loose flap of skin under the chin of certain animals

NB: Though not quite homophones, when used in such a phrase as "wattle and daub," the "t" of "wattle" sounds virtually identical to the "d" of "waddle."

wade – walk in shallow water; (fig.) w. "into," deliberately enter a controversy

weighed – measured mass of an object; hefted; balanced; considered (*w. the pros and cons*)

wail – (v., n.) moan, cry, keen

wale – ridge, as in corduroy cloth

whale – cetaceous aquatic mammal; (fig.) anything huge in scope (*w. of a sale*)

wain – wagon; cart

wane – ebb, diminish

waist – midsection of the body, between the torso and legs

> **waste** – (v.) use profligately; misuse; (n.)
> unused part; trash; (adj.) remaining after
> manufacture, usu. of no value (*w. product*)

wait – (v.) bide one's time; pend; (w. "on") serve as a waiter, as in a restaurant;
(n.) period of time before an action
or activity (*a long w.*)

> **weight** – heft, mass, poundage; (fig.)
> consideration, deliberation

waited – p. tense of "wait"

> **weighted** – p. tense of "weight";
> recalculated to include external, non-
> germane factors (*w. average*)

waive – give up, as a right

> **wave** – (v.) signal by hand; greet silently;
> (n.) upswelling of water by tidal or
> other forces; any similar movement
> (*sound w.*); increase, cycle (*w. of support*)

waiver – ceding of a right or penalty; authorization to proceed; variance

> **waver** – hesitate, go back and forth
> between options; teeter

want – (v.) desire, lack; (n.) need   **wont** – habit, custom

war – battle; armed fight; state of formal antagonism between opposing nations,
peoples, etc.; any conflict (*at w. with
oneself*)

> **wore** – had on, dressed in; eroded (*w.
> away*); lasted (*w. well*); used up (*w. out*);
> diminished resistance (*w. down*)

ward – (v.) (w. "off") avert; (n.) protégé, minor dependent; orphan; political
division, usu. in a city (*w. heeler*)

> **warred** – fought, engaged in battle

ware – type of goods (*hardw.*); usu. pl. when used alone

> **wear** – have on, dress oneself in; erode,
> eat away; last well

> **where** – adverb indicating location or
> direction; (with "to") whither; (with
> "from") whence

warn – threaten; alert (to danger or consequences)

> **worn** – (v.) had on; (adj.) tired out,
> exhausted; threadbare; eroded

wart – virus-caused skin growth; shortcoming, imperfection; (pl.) (*w. and all*)

> **wort** – malt liquid used in fermentation;
> any of various herbs used in
> medicinal compounds

wary – cautious; skeptical

> **wherry** – light rowboat; barge used to
> transport freight

wat – temple (Thailand)

> **watt** – unit of electric measurement
>
> **wot** – knew (arch.)

wax – (v.) grow, expand; (n.) material from secretions of bees used for candle-
making; secretion in the ear canal

> **whacks** – (v.) hits, pummels; cuts with
> a heavy blade; (n.) hits; slashes

way – direction; manner, style

> **weigh** – measure mass or weight
>
> **whey** – skim from making cheese

we – personal pronoun indicating first person plural: two or more individuals;
collectively, one's partner, family,
compatriots, or other group

> **oui** – yes (Fr.)
>
> **wee** – small, tiny (ch. Scot.) (*w. bairn*)
>
> **whee** – (exclam.) word of glee or joy

weak – paltry, ineffectual

> **week** – period of seven days

weal – common good, welfare; body politic, wealth

> **we'll** – (contr.) we will, we shall
>
> **wheel** – (v.) roll; spin; (n.) tire; circular,
> spindled hub for turning (*potter's w.*)
> or directing motion (*steering w.*)

wear – see *ware, where*

weather – (v.) age; expose to the elements; survive (*w. a storm*); (n.) local climate
condition or phenomenon (*today's w.*)

> **wether** – male sheep, usu. castrated,
> that leads the flock (*bellw.*)
>
> **whether** – (adv.) if; in case that

weave – interlace; create cloth using a loom; tell or make up a tale

                  we've – (contr.) we have

we'd – (contr.) we would   **weed** – (v.) remove unwanted plants,
                                  behavior, etc. (*w. out*); (n.) any
                                  unwanted plant in a garden

weir – dam; lock in a canal used to raise or lower water levels

                  we're – (contr.) we are

weld – (v.) fuse pieces of metal by heating, oft. with alloys; (n.) such a fusion;
                                  variety of flower yielding a yellow
                                  dye; that or similar dye

                  welled – bubbled up; flew, gushed forth;
                                  amassed (*her eyes w. with tears*)

wen – cyst; benign tumor; hard growth on the skin

                  when – at what time; simultaneous
                                  with, while; although, whereas

wench – serving girl, barmaid; lower-class girl (archaic)

                  winch – (v., n.) hoist, crank

were – p. tense of "was"; existed   **whirr** – (v.) turn, spin, with a buzzing or
                                  whooshing sound; (n) such a sound

wet – (v.) dampen, moisten; (adj.) damp; (w. "all") ridiculous; (n.) supporter of
                                  alcohol sales (obs.)

                  whet – hone, sharpen; increase

when – at what time; while; (fig.) although, whereas

                  wen – cyst; benign tumor; hard growth
                                  on the skin

where – see *ware, wear*

which – (pron.) one of several alternatives; previously mentioned; that; (adj.) in
                                  queries, referring to what one(s) of
                                  several possibilities is meant

                  witch – Wiccan; practitioner of magic;
                                  crone; virago, shrew (sl.)

NB: Traditionally, in American English, "which" is recommended for nonrestrictive clauses, which are set off by commas and can be omitted without affecting the clarity of a sentence. "That" is preferred for restrictive clauses that introduce essential information. In British and Canadian English, "which" is often used for nonrestrictive clauses.

Whig – 19th-century Am. political party   **wig** – false hair; toupée; perruke

while – (v.) (w. "away") pass time idly; (n.) a nonspecifed period of time (*all the w.*); (adv.) when; simultaneously; (conj.) as; during a specific period

        wile – trick; artifice; stratagem; guile (usu. pl., as "wiles")

whin – basalt stone; thorny gorse shrub **win** – succeed; take first place

whine – complain, usu. in a childish, nagging voice

        wine – fermented drink from grapes

whined – complained, griped   **wind** – coil, as on a spool; loop around, as a mountain road; w. "up," bring to an end; create tension, as with a spring-operated toy

        wined – entertained; hosted, usu. as an enticement (*w. and dined*)

whirled – turned in circles; twirled; turned suddenly (*w. around*)

        world – Earth; any planet that might contain life; (fig.) community (*in my w.*); profession (*the art w.*)

whirred – hummed, made a whirring sound; ran smoothly

        word – identifying term; sequence of letters denoting meaning; verdict, opinion guidance; for Christians, the Bible (*God's w.*)

whit – small bit; iota   **wit** – sense, sanity; intelligence; sense of humor; amusing person; wag, jokester

white – in painting, combination of all colors in equal ratios; (fig.) pure, good, untainted, heroic (*w. knight*)

        wight – specter; ghost; haunt

Many words beginning "wh" are actually pronounced as if the first two letters were reversed to "hw": the "h" is apirated before the "w" is enunciated. Most of their counterparts without an "h"—"wen," "wile," "witch," etc.—are therefore not exact homophones; they are listed herein primarily to ensure precision in spelling. An example is "wither": whether used as a singular verb or the collective noun "withers," it sounds different from "whither" but is close enough to be listed.

whither – where to; in what direction or place; opp. of "whence"

>**wither** – (v.) shrivel, dry up; languish; die on the vine
>
>(**withers**) – (collective n.) ridge between the shoulder blades of a horse, dog, etc.; commonly used to measure height

whoa – (interj.) stop, halt   **woe** – sorrow; grief; self-pity (*w. is me*)

whole – (adj.) complete, entire; undivided; (n.) entirety, sum of all parts

>**hole** – opening, aperture

wholly – entirely, completely; utterly   **holey** – full of holes

>**holy** – sacred, revered

whop – (v.) hit, beat; (n.) hard blow   **wop** – vulgar, offensive term for a person of Italian heritage (sl.)

who's – (contr.) who is   **whose** – poss. of "who"; belonging to; originating from (*W. idea was this?*)

why – for what reason or cause   **wye** – the letter "Y"; intersection, graph, or other object of that shape

>**Wye** – a river in England

why's – reasons, rationales   **wise** – (n., collective) learned, intelligent people; sages; (adj.) sage, insightful; sarcastic, smart-mouthed (*w. remarks*)

wind – see *whined*; see also (p. 110) *wend*, in "Easily Misused, Confused, or Mistyped Words"

windlass – winch; crank, as for raising or lowering a well-bucket

>**windless** – without wind, still

wood – forest; grove; organic fibrous tissue of a tree or shrub; type of golf club

>**would** – will; wish; prefer (*w. it were so*); cond. mood of "will"

worst – (v.) defeat a foe; best; outdo (n.) least desired outcome (*fear the w.*); (adj.) superlative of "bad"; least favorable

>**wurst** – sausage (Ger.); in English, usu. in combination, e.g.,. bratwurst, blutwurst, liverwurst, etc.

wrack – see *rack*

wrap, wrapped – see *rap, rapt*

wreak – see *reek*

wretch – see *retch*

wring – see *ring*

write – inscribe; create, as a manuscript or correspondence; (fig.) send a letter

> **right** – (v.) correct, emend; adjust; re-establish stability (*r. the ship of state*); (n.) guaranteed privilege; inherent liberty or authority (*divine r. of kings*); (fig.) conservative political bloc; (adj.) correct, not wrong; opp. of "left"; just, fair
>
> **rite** – ceremony, ritual
>
> **wright** – craftsman, artisan (*playw.*)

wrote – penned, inscribed

> **rote** – learning style using repetition; memorization (*learn by r.*)

X

xenia – process of cross-pollinating plants to introduce foreign characteristics, leading to hybrid offspring

> **Xenia** – township in Ohio
>
> **zinnia** – genus of flowering annual plants

NB: I had nearly given up on discovering any "x" or "z" words with homophones in English—until I remembered "Xenia." I thought at once of its almost-homophonic mate, the zinnia, which refers to both the common name and an entire genus of annual flowers named for German botanist J. G. Zinn. "Xenia" properly has a longer "e" sound than the short "i" of the flower, but many Americans, especially in the South and Midwest, conversationally call the flowers "ZEEN-yuz." So we err on the side of inclusion—and completing the alphabet.

Y

yack – talk unceasingly, gab

yawl – two-masted sailboat

yawn – inhale w. fatigue; gape

yak – oxlike bovine of central Asia

y'all – (colloq.) you all; those present

yon – yonder, over there; far away (usu. idiomatically, e.g., *hither and y.*)

yay – (exclam.) hooray   **yea** – yes, aye; assent (in a recorded vote)

yew – evergreen tree or shrub, genus *Taxus*, often used as a hedge; wood used
for an archer's bow

ewe – female sheep

you – second person; one addressed

yews – pl. of "yew"; small trees or shrubs of the genus *Taxus*

ewes – pl. of "ewe"

use – utilize; avail

youse – irreg. pl. of "you" (sl., ch. NY
and Boston metropolitan regions)

yoke – (v.) harness, esp. constraining oxen or horses; constrain; (n.) harness,
constraint; (fig.) burden

yolk – part of an egg; embryo protein

you'll – (contr.) you will   **Yule** – midwinter holiday and festival
corresponding with winter solstice,
of pagan Germanic origin, later
incorporated into Christian worship;
Noel; Christmastime

you're – (contr.) you are   **your** – possessive of "you"; belonging
to the one addressed

(yore) – mythical past (*days of y.*)

youse – see *use, ewes, yews*

Z

zinnia – genus of flowering annual plants

xenia – process of cross-pollinating plants
to introduce foreign characteristics,
leading to hybrid offspring

Xenia – a township in Ohio

Easily Misused, Confused, or Mistyped Words

English begs, borrows, and steals words from every language on earth. "Bistro," meaning a café, derives from the Russian word meaning "quickly," and "café" is the French word for "coffee" (which derives from the Turkish "qawha," apparently named for the "kaffa" area of Ethiopia where the plant originates). "Sheik" is Arabic; "qi" is Chinese, "data" Latin, and "tarantula" Spanish; the word "language" itself came to us via French from the Latin "lingua," meaning "tongue."

Americans adopt those words and adapt them to our pronunciation models, often making their meaning unclear. To write correctly, it's important to know how they should be pronounced so we don't end up choosing the wrong word. Sometimes pronunciation knowledge isn't enough: "sheik" most closely rhymes with "flake," and "chic" with "leak," but many people pronounce both words as if they were spelled "sheek." So you have to know which word to use, because when you type them, most spell-checker software can only recognize that both words are correct; it cannot figure out which one you meant.

Many of the words in the following list are similar in either spelling or meaning, but some are very different: just a little juggling turns "amulet" into "emulate." Anyone with keyboarding experience knows how easy it is to type the wrong word when thoughts move faster than fingers (or vice versa); this list won't speed up the slower of the two, but it might help you catch errors before it's too late—say, when it's already in print and you have egg on your face.

Some typos, of course, are just typos; they reflect not ignorance but misunderstanding (and "misunderstanding" is not the same as "incomprehension"). A copy editor in an advertising agency described an embarrassing typo—actually a mondegreen (see p. 133)—that he caught just in time: a copywriter had typed "pre-Madonna" instead of "prima donna." An online ad, unfortunately not caught in time, described a New York apartment as a "specious 6-room condo" rather than as a "spacious" one—which in the NY real estate market, which sometimes counts a closet as a room, might be perfectly accurate.

But take comfort: it's not just the "little people" who make such mistakes. Writing in *The New York Times* on June 6, 2011, journalist Elizabeth Rosenthal quoted a scientist regarding an *E. coli* outbreak. She wrote that, according to her source, signs of infection can sometimes be missed. "Dr. Tauxe [said], 'You can go to a place wreaking of chlorine, and find nothing.'" Though *E. coli* might be wreaking havoc on peoples' lives, she meant "reeking," i.e., with an acrid odor.

A week later Chris Tomlinson of the Associated Press wrote, "'The problem is that some out-of-state e-retailers openly flaunt the law,' said Texas state Democratic Rep. Elliot Naishtat." In this case, it's impossible to know whether it was the reporter or the representative who used "flaunt" instead of "flout," but Tomlinson's editor clearly did a less than thorough job on the story.

In my hometown newspaper a reporter described a house featured in the "Living" section one summer (July 2, 2011): "Just off the deck is another scarlet red oak leviathan that *reins* majestically over the lot... To keep the *site* lines uncluttered, he installed a telescoping down draft in back of the gas range." [emphases added] He meant, of course, a tree that "reigns" over the lot, and that the owner wanted clear "sight" lines; once again, the computer spell-checker's shortcomings—or those of an editor or proofreader—were there for all to see.

Such descriptives as these are often tricky for writers. Red oaks are of the species *Quercus*, variety *rubrus* (Latin for "red"), and a red oak is different from a white oak, a chestnut oak, a live oak, and a pin oak. But calling a red oak "scarlet" seems redundant, even if it is properly descriptive—especially as there is yet another variety of oak trees called "scarlet oak."

As for "leviathan," it's a biblical word for a sea monster, familiar to many of us from Herman Melville's *Moby-Dick*. Figuratively it can refer to anything huge and powerful—and usually animate—but most of us would simply call that scarlet red oak leviathan a "huge red oak." Exept Southerners like me, who might prefer "a big ol' oak tree."

Three years later (Oct. 8, 2014) the same newspaper featured a house owned by a carpenter and builder who created a dining table "made from old door jams." I wondered which flavor his family prefers when they eat buttered toast: strawberry, apricot, or blackberry "jamb."

On June 20, 2015, an online political newsletter (*PoliticsNC*) correctly cited its definition of the phrase "quid pro quo," highlighted during the impeachment of Donald J. Trump. The Latin was correct, as was the definition ... but the author cited the "Miriam Webster" dictionary as his source, as if Noah's wife Miriam was the power behind his throne. (For those under 50, Noah Webster published his *An American Dictionary of the English Language* in 1828; the Merriam brothers bought the rights to it after his death in 1843, and the company is still today called Merriam-Webster.)

Some word phrases also function as words: "any one" and "anyone" both are correct in different circumstances, as are "a while" and "awhile" and "any time" and "anytime." The latter can be confusing: "Any time you want to go is good with me" is an adverbial use of a two-word adjective-plus-noun phrase. But early in the 20th century a popular phrase was "an anytime girl," referring to a young (or not-so-young) lady who was available for a date with anyone who asked. That usage is an adjectival descriptive. Today, "any time" is standard, while "anytime" is not, though it still exists as a colloquialism. Just be careful which you choose to use.

We've seen (p. 48) that "lead" can rhyme with either "bed" or "seed." That makes "lead" a homograph (meaning "written the same"); but "lead" and "led" are homophones (written differently, they sound the same). In this case the meanings differ according to how the word is pronounced and how it is spelled. A leader leads, but yesterday the leader led. The word that *rhymes* with "led," but which is *spelled* "lead," is a heavy metal. That's why the space between lines in printed books is called "leading," pronounced "LED-ng": it refers to the width of the leaden bars that were traditionally used to separate one line of type from the next. "LED-ng" and "LEED-ing" are homographs (both written as "leading") but are not homophones. Again, you have to know which word you want and make sure you type it correctly when you write, and pronounce it correctly when you speak.

Remember also that the order of words makes a difference in their meaning, sometimes dramatically. "The measures were held up by court rulings" is very different from—in practice almost the opposite of—"the measures were upheld by court rulings." The first means "delayed"; the second indicates ratification.

We are all—students, teachers, writers, editors, publishers—occasionally susceptible to making an embarrassing solecism (which is not the same as solipsism). The following list comprises more than seven hundred words that trip us up, so make certain you choose the one you really intend to use. A few of them, whose confusion arises almost exclusively from their use in idioms, have brief definitions appended. I hope the list is found useful by every reader of this book.

a while (n.)	awhile (adv.)	
abbess	abyss	
abet	abut	
abode	adobe	
accept	except	expect
access	excess	
accolade	allocate	
acidulous	assiduous	
acquisitive	inquisitive	
adapt	adopt	adept
addition	edition	
adventuress	adventurous	
adverse	averse	
adverse	inverse	obverse
affect	effect	
agnostic	agonistic	
all ready (adj.)	already (adv.)	
allude	elude	
allusion	elision	illusion
(also see *elusion*)		
alumna (f.)	alumnus (m.)	
alumnae (f. pl.)	alumni (m. or mixed pl.)	
amend	emend	
amoral	immoral	
amulet	emulate	
anecdote	antidote	
any more (adj.)	anymore (adv.)	
any one (adj.)	anyone (pron.)	
any time (n., adv.)	anytime (adj.) (irreg.)	
any way (n.)	anyway (adv.)	
apostle	epistle	
appreciable	appreciative	
argot	ergo	ergot
artesian	artisan	
assume	presume	

assure	ensure	insure
atone	attune	
aureole	oriole	
baklava	balaclava	
baron	barren	
baroness	barrenness	
baroque	barque	
basal	basil	
bases	basis	
basest	bassist	
Bataan	baton	batten
bath	bathe	
behest	bequest	request
belay	belie	
bellow	below	
bollix	bollocks	
brasserie	brassiere	brazier
breath	breathe	
bundt	bunt	
bunt	punt	
cache	cachet	
Cain	cane	cayenne
caliber	caliper	
Calvary	cavalry	
canapé	canopy	
capital	capitol	
carve	crave	
cask	casket	casque
casual	causal	
catch	ketch	kvetch
catsup	catch up	ketchup
caution	cushion	
celebrity	celerity	celery
champing (at the bit)	chomping	
chantey	shanty	shandy

chard	shard	
chauffeur	shofar	
cinch	sync	
clef	cleft	cliff
cliff	Clift (name)	
coalition	collision	collusion
cockle	cuckold*	
coffer	coiffure	
coma	comma	
commensurate (adj.)	commiserate (v.)	
complacent	complaisant	
complementary	complimentary	
concede	conceit	
conferees	confreres	
confidant (m.)	confidante (f.)	confident
confirm	conform	
congenial	congenital	
conservation	conversation	
considerably	considerately	
console	consul	
contend	content	
convey	convoy	
co-op	co-opt	
corporal	corporeal	
coven	covey	convoy
craven	graven	
dais	lectern	podium
(the platform speakers sit on)	(what they stand behind)	
(what they step onto)		
deceased	diseased	

---

* The late, great Canadian author Robertson Davies tossed off a delightful, and deliberate, solecism in his superb novel, *World of Wonders*. Magnus Eisengrim, a sleight-of-hand magician, quotes another character describing an experience that had "warmed the cuckolds of her heart."

defer	deter	
defiantly	definitely	
defuse	diffuse	
demean	demesne	domain
demur	demure	
dent	dint	
deter	detour	
devaluation	devolution	
disburse	disperse	
disillusion	dissolution	
disinterested	uninterested	
duad	duet	dyad
egoist	egotist	
elegy	eulogy	
elicit	illicit	
elude	evade	
eliminate	illuminate	
elusion	illusion	
emigrate	immigrate	
eminent	immanent	imminent
emollient	emolument	
empirical	imperial	
endemic	pandemic	
ensure	insure	assure
entomology	etymology*	
epic	epoch	
erotic	erratic	
estuary	ossuary	
-eval (medieval, primeval)	Evel (Knievel, stunt driver and daredevil)	
	evil	
exacerbate	exasperate	exaggerate
expansive	expensive	

---

* People who can't distinguish between "entomology" and "etymology" bug me in ways I can't put into words. (tweet from Tal Waterhouse, @iiTalW, May 2, 2018

facts	fax	
fa′-ker	fa-kir′ (*alt. sp.* "fakeer")	
fallacious	fellatio	
fallow	fellow	follow
farther	further	
Fauré	foray	
fêted	fetid	
fiend	friend	
finally	finely	
fiscal	physical	
flamenco	flamingo	
flange	phalange	
flaunt	flout	
for•bear′	fore′•bear	
fort	forte*	
frantic	frenetic	
friend	fried	
furl	furrow	
gambit	gamut	
gantlet (what you throw down)	gauntlet (what you run)	
garish	garnish	
garret	garotte	
gesture	jester	
gird	grid	
genteel	gentile	gentle
gluten	glutton	
gorilla	guerrilla	
Grand Am	grande dame	
gravelly	gravely	

---

*This word, meaning "strength" or "area of expertise," derives from the French "forte," with a silent "e," which means "strong"; it is not rooted in the Italian forté, meaning "loud" (as in pianoforté or fortepiano). However, almost every American (mis)pronounces it "for-TAY"; in a few more editions of this book, the "correct" spelling might have to be given up as a lost cause.

gristle	grizzle	
grisly	gristly	grizzly
groove	grove	
gumption	gumshoe	
hallowed	hollowed	
hankers	hunkers	
hearsay	heresy	
Hippocratic	hypocritical	hypercritical
historic	historical	
historical	hysterical	
home (in on)	hone (sharpen, as a knife)	
homey	homely	
homely	homily	
homily	hominy	
immanent	imminent	eminent
immoral	immortal	amoral
immorality	immortality	
immunity	impunity	
imperial	imperil	
impinge	infringe	
implication	inference	
imply	infer	
impugn	impute	
in to	in two	into
inanity	insanity	
incest	insist	
inconsonant	inconstant	incontinent
inclement	increment	
indent/ed	intend/ed	
indigent	indignant	
indignation	indignity	
indolence	insolence	
inequity	iniquity	
ingenious	ingenuous	
install	instill	

intelligence	intelligentsia	
inter	intern	
intercepted	intersected	
interstate	intestate	
inveigh	inveigle	
jalousie	jealousy	
ken	kin	
ketch	kvetch	kitsch
lath (slat of wood)	lathe (tool)	
lay (present)	laid (past)	laid (participle)
lie (present)	lay (past)	lain (participle)
leach	leash	
league	liege	
lectern (see *dais*)	podium	dais
legislator	legislature	
lend/lent	loan/loaned	
lentil	lintel	
less	lest	list
lessee	lesser	lessor
lore	lower	
loose	lose	
loud	lout	
Madison	medicine	
magnate	magnet	
malaise	malice	
malicious*	militias*	
manager	manger	
marine	moreen	moiré
marital	martial	
mewed	mooed	

---

*These two words are about as close as one can get to homophony without quite being homophones. Heard in certain contexts, they can work as a mondegreen [see p. 133]: "The cause of the explosion in Ukraine is uncertain: Was it malicious, or was it militias?"

menstrual	minstrel	
mirth	myrrh	
mnemonic	pneumonic	
moor	more	
moot	mute	
moral	morale	
motif	motive	
mustard* ("cut the mustard")	muster* ("pass muster")	
nocturn (part of matins)	nocturne (painting, music composition)	
nougat	nugget	
ochre	okra	
occident	oxidant	
onyx	oryx	
ordinance	ordnance	
parameter	perimeter	
parish	perish	
parodying	parroting	
Pasteur	pastor	pasture
pastiche	pasticcio	pistachio
pastoral (adj.)	pastorale (n.)	
pawned	pond	
pen	pin	
penchant	pension	
penultimate	ultimate	prepenultimate
perpetrate	perpetuate	

---

* "Muster" is a verb or noun referring to the gathering of troops in readiness for battle. It has come to mean, figuratively, to meet expectations; hence something that can "pass muster" is good enough. "Mustard" is a savory green whose seeds are used in cooking or ground into a condiment. In the 19th century the phrase "keen as mustard" commonly referred to an attribute of zestiness, and writer O. Henry first wrote the phrase "cut the mustard" in a short story—possibly to mean the real article, in the opinion of word expert Michael Quinion (from his website WorldWideWords.org). So while *"pass muster"* and *"cut the mustard"* mean almost the same thing, don't confuse them: if you pass the mustard, you're probably talking about Grey Poupon.

perquisite	prerequisite	
persecute	prosecute	
persevere	perverse	preserve
persona	personal	personnel
petrel	petrol	
phase	phrase	
physics	psychics	physique
pike ("come down the pike")	pipe (not "come down the pipe")	
pilfer (steal)	rifle (poke around, search through)	
plaid	played	
plaintiff	plaintive	
pneumonic	mnemonic	
podium (see *dais*)	dais	lectern
pommel	pummel	
popery	potpourri	
populace	populist	populous
poser	poseur	
precede	proceed	
predominant	predominate	
premier	premiere	
prescribe	proscribe	
preview	purview	
principal	principle	
procrastinate	prognosticate	
prodigal	protocol	
prodigy	protégé	
prophecy	prophesy	
profit	prophet	
prone	supine	
prostate	prostrate	
protean	protein	
provenance	providence	
punt	bunt	
quail	quell	
querulous	quizzical	

rappel	repel	
read-out	redoubt	
rebel	revel	
recess	recession	
reflects	reflex	
regal	regale	
regard	regards	
regime	regimen	regiment
reserve	reverse	
revelation	revolution	devolution
rogue	rouge	
sale	sell	
saliva	salvia	
satire	satyr	
scrimmage	skirmish	
scrip	script	
sedate	serene	
seminal	Seminole	
septic	styptic	
service	surface	
shudder	shutter	
sigh	sci (sci-fi)	psy (psy-ops)
silver	sliver	
solecism	solipsism	
sooth	soothe	
spacious	specious	
spoor	spore	
splurge	spurge	surge
stanch	staunch	
starlet	starlit	
stent	stint	
supposably	supposedly	
synapses	synopses	
sync	cinch	
taffy	toffee	

tambour	tambourine	timbre
tartar	Tatar	'tater
tempera	tempura	
tenant	tenet	
tenor	tenure	
than	then	thin
timber	timbre	
toe the line (not "tow")	tow	
tough	though	thought
	through	trough
tortious	tortuous	torturous
Tourette (Syndrome)	turret	
trail	trial	
trawl	troll	
turbid	turgid	
udder	utter	
urban	urbane	
uvea	uvula	
venal	venial	
verbatim	verboten	
verge	virgin	Virgil
vice	vise	
vicious	viscous	
vigil	vigilance	visual
violent	violet	
waddle	wattle	
wanton	wonton	
warp	wrap	
wary	weary	
wench	wrench	
wend	wind*	

---

*In some dialects, "wind" with a short "i" is a near homophone for "wend";
however, its homograph, spelled the same ("wind") but pronounced with a long
"i," is a homophone for "whined" and "wined."

whelk	whelp	
whined	wind*	
who's	whose	
worse	worst	wurst
wrack	wreck	
wreck/wrecked (a car)	wreak/wreaked (havoc) or "wrought" havoc)	

More confusing words...

Frequently
Mispronounced Words

Many words in English are pronounced incorrectly by even the most educated speakers. In some cases, a word that is familiar in the written form isn't often used in speech, so the person hasn't heard it pronounced properly. Some words are commonly mispronounced by public speakers who should know better (teachers, actors, "expert" guest speakers) as well as those who have no particular reason to (politicians and other public figures with no formal training in language). In my case, an elder brother mistaught me, to my later embarrassment, that a gangster's moll (rhymes with "doll") was pronounced "mole," and that "mien" (sounds like "mean") was pronounced like "mane." Being an admiring younger brother, I accepted his knowledge as gospel ... until I realized he was as fallible as I was gullible.

There are many ways to learn and remember correct pronunciations. Sometimes the origin of the word offers a clue: "cachet" and "cache" are French words, so the "ch" is soft in both ("sh," not "tch"); but the "-et" at the end of "cachet" gives it that very French final syllable of "AY," while the plain, unaccented final "e" of "cache" is silent, like the "e" in "house." "Short-lived" means something has a short life, and that long "i" carries through from the noun to the adjective, as it does in "lively." In some cases a mnemonic—a phonic memory aid—is useful. The first mnemonic I learned as a child was that stalactites, with a "c" in the middle, grow downward from the ceiling of a cave, while stalagmites, with a "g," grow up from the ground.

This short list only skims the surface of the ocean of mispronounced words— an ocean that grows deeper with every cohort of graduates who haven't been taught correctly. But for those who do want to learn to speak standard English, here's another option: learn these, and many, many others, by rote, also known as old-fashioned memorization (and not to be confused with "wrote").

Word	**does** sound like	does **not** sound like
ask	task	tax
bade	lad	made
cache	rash	catch
cachet	sashay	hatchet
clique	meek	flick
coup de grâce*	rood: a cross	soup *or* bra
("p" is silent; "ce" is pronounced)		
err	purr	pair
forte**	sport	today
herb	urb-an ("h" is silent)	her
often	soften ("t" is silent)	cough ten
pique	leak	sick
sheik	flake	chic
short-lived	dived	give
wainscot	lot or cut	coat

---

* Though people sometimes portray the *coup de grâce* as a cruel, final indignity, it is actually the opposite: the genteel, even elegant end to suffering in a duel or fight. It might be quickly cutting an enemy's throat or stabbing him through the heart; in either case it is used to end his suffering, not prolong it. Its technical translation is "a stroke of grace."

** See note, p. 104.

Commonly Misspelled & Misspoken Words—& Eggcorns

Many words that we might think of as homophones aren't: they're simply common misspellings of real words. Some are foreign words or phrases that have been adopted into English; others are traditional English words that have been bastardized to match similar words with different orthography. For example, "lax" is a real Middle English word that means "loose" or "non-rigorous"; it derives from Latin "laxus" and before that Indo-European "leg-" meaning "slack." "Lackadaisical" has a completely different origin but in some usages has a similar meaning of "listless," "languid," "lacking spirit." Too many people change "lackadaisical" to "lax-adaisical."

In a different vein, a "chaise longue" in French means a "long chair," and it's pronounced "shayz long"; but many Americans call it (and spell it) a chaise "lounge." That might be because "longue" and "lounge" share the same letters, though in a different order—or maybe because we like to lounge around in chaises longues.

According to the most recent edition of Merriam-Webster's *New World College Dictionary*, either of the above usages could be categorized as an "eggcorn": a neologism defined as an incorrect word or phrase that has some feasible logic behind it (similar to a mondegreen). Webster's cites such usages as "spreading like wildflowers" in place of "spreading like wildfire" and "cold slaw" for "cole slaw" as being plausibly logical or sensible.

There are also many words in American English that are fairly common but that people simply spell incorrectly, or get confused about. A friend who worked at an advertising agency shared this true story: "On days when our agency has pizza delivered," he writes, "someone marks each box to identify its contents. This was on one box today: Glutton-free." That description might be true of dry toast or even gluten-free muffins, and more recently even of pizza ... but it's unlikely to describe those who order it in every week.

The very first example in the list that follows is a Latin phrase, "ad hominem," often misspoken and occasionally mistyped as "ad homonym." The reason for the confusion is that the phrase, written correctly, is from classical Latin, a language that few Americans study today; contrarily, the word "homonym" derives from ancient Greek, which even fewer have learned (and which is quite different from modern spoken Greek). So here's a quick lesson about both ancient tongues.

Greek cheat sheet

"Homonym" is an honest-to-goodness English word meaning, among other things, "homophone," found in the title of this book: a word with the same pronunciation as another but a different meaning. "Homonym" derives from the Greek words "homos," meaning "same," and "onyma," meaning "name": thus "same name." Other words with the "homos" root are "homograph" (same writing, or spelled the same); "homogenized" (of the same texture, blend, etc. from "homos" and "genus," meaning "kind" or "sort"); and, of course, "homophone," (from "homos" and "phonos," or sound). Familiar words that use the "onyma" or "nym" ("name") root include "synonym" ("syn" meaning "together with"), "antonym" ("anti" meaning "against"), "pseudonym" ("pseudo" meaning "false"), and "anonymous" ("ano" meaning "without").

By recognizing these Greek root words—*anti, genus, homo, onyma* (or *nym*), *phonos, pseudo, syn*—and others that are common in English, you'll find it easier to recognize the English words they contribute to—and you'll be far closer to remembering how to use, as well as how to spell, modern words derived from them. Thinking about "phonos" alone, you can come up with "stereophonic" (three-dimensional sound); "telephone" (far-away sound); "phonics" (the study of sounds); "phonetics" (the study of spoken speech); and "phonograph" (sound that's inscribed, or written, as on a phonograph record). If you think of "syn" plus the Greek word for time, "chronos," you get "synchronize." It's not hard, once you understand the principles and methods involved, and then the words "homograph," "homonym," and "homophone" make perfect sense.

BUT ...

The phrase "ad hominem" is not Greek at all, it's Latin, and it doesn't have anything to do with the sounds of words. As you will see, it refers to a personal attack, differentiating it from an argument against someone's ideas or the subject under discussion.

<u>Latin cheat sheet</u>

Latin (like Greek) takes nouns, pronouns, and adjectives and changes them according to their use in a sentence (that is, the words "decline," creating "declensions"). The subject of a sentence acts on the verb, while the direct object is acted upon. The object of a preposition ("to," "from," "with," "between," etc.) will take one of several forms according to whether the preposition indicates direct action, indirect action, possession, comparison, description, or other characteristics.

As a result, using nouns in different ways causes them to appear in different forms, or cases; Latin has seven cases, of which the five primary ones are Nominative, Genitive (or Possessive), Dative, Accusative, and Ablative. The five cases of the word for woman, "femina," are *femina, feminae, feminae, feminam,* and *femina.* The word for "man" in Latin is "homo"; it starts as *homo* (the man [acts]); then becomes *hominis* (of or belonging to the man); *homini* (to the man); *hominem* (directly at/against/toward the man); and *homine* (compared to, than, or from the man).

So an argument directed at the man is an *argumentam ad hominem*—where the preposition "ad" means "against" and requires the accusative form "hominem." Say someone makes an assertion or expresses an opinion ("The sky is green."). Instead of correcting the facts ("No, it's blue.") or challenging the opinion ("Where's the evidence?"), an *ad hominem* argument attacks the speaker ("You're an idiot.").

Thus it's considered both demeaning to the maker of the argument and meaningless in countering the original position. It is often effective, simply because people are prone to enjoy hearing a person put down, but it is not, and will never be, an argument "ad homonym."

<u>Back to the list</u>

Some of the words and phrases in the following listing are mispronounced, misspelled, misunderstood, or all three. Some are Latin- or Greek-derived; others are Germanic, or have other linguistic origins (even Sanskrit). But wherever the words or the roots that make them up came from, you should beware of them all, and try to learn the correct usages by heart. The correct usage is on the left column below; incorrect spelling and usage(s)—errors to avoid—appear on the right.

<u>Correct</u>	<u>Incorrect</u>
ad hominem	ad <u>homonym</u>
ad nauseam	ad nause<u>u</u>m

Correct	Incorrect
all right	alright
beaucoup	boocoup *or* bookoos
beaux	beaus
bellwether	bellweather
bloodcurdling	bloodcurling
blowhard	blow heart
brouhaha	brewhaha
cellphone	self phone
chaise longue	chaise lounge
chimney	chimbley
cole slaw	cold slaw
come to naught	come to not
courtesy call	curtsey call
crème brûlée	cream brulee
crème de cacao	crème de cocoa *or* cream de cacao
crème de menthe	crème de mint *or* cream de mint
cut and dried	cut and dry
cut the mustard	cut the muster
doctoral	doctorial
en masse	on mass
entrepreneur	enterpreneur
especially	eckspecially
fait accomplis	fate accomplis
February	Febuary
foment (hatred)	forment (hatred)
hare-brained	hair-brained*
heyday	hay day
home in on	hone in on
horehound	hoarhound *or* whorehound
in memoriam	in memorium
infinitesimal	infantesmal

---

*Some blonde jokes could be considered hair-brained, but that might be one bad pun too many for some readers.

Correct	Incorrect
lackadaisical	lacksadaisical *or* laxadaisical
(a new) lease on life	(a new) leash on life
leeway	leadway
leitmotif	light motif *or* light motive
library	liberry
linchpin	lynchpin
martial arts	marital arts
minuscule	miniscule
mischievous	mischievious
nerve-wracking	nerve-wrecking
nether regions	never regions
nip in the bud	nip in the butt
nuclear	nucular
pass muster	pass mustard
pastoral	pastorial
rack and ruin	wreck and ruin
restaurateur	restauranteur
(a long) row to hoe	(a long) road to hoe
sauerkraut	sourkraut
set foot in	step foot in*
give short shrift to	give short shift to
smorgasbord	smorgasboard *or* smorgasborg
supersede	supercede
ubiquitous	ubiquitious
vocal cords	vocal chords

---

*This usage is becoming so common that it is almost standard; traditionalists like me still strongly prefer "set" to "step."

More misspelled and mispronounced words

Neologisms

William Shakespeare was one of the greatest coiners of words in the history of the English language. In our information age, innovative businesses are among the most prolific generators of neologisms ("neo" meaning "new," and "logos" meaning "word," with the suffix "ism" indicating usage). Such terms as "etail," "iPod," and "eBook" are altogether new, while "mac" and "twitter" and many other words have gained new meanings from being adopted and adapted by technology companies. In the early 2010s the words "staycation" and "playcation" appeared; the first seems likely to survive the long-term dictionary screening process, the latter less so—but both already have clear meanings in the travel industry.

The following words do not officially exist in the English language—at least in dictionaries—at least not yet—though I've come across them all, some spoken, others written in newspapers or on blogs, in online comment sections, or elsewhere. They're all trying to be real words but somehow go off the mark. Some of them are quite charming, and maybe someday they'll become familiar and accepted enough to enter the language. For now they're illegitimate, but if any of them appeals to you strongly (as some do to me), try them out; maybe with regular, widespread use, they will become standardized.

I've marked with a heart (♥) the neologisms I particularly like. When you encounter others, share them with me: they might show up in a future edition.

Not-quite words	Purported meanings
allegator®	one who makes allegations
NB: trademarked by Media Watch at Daily Kos	
beauticious	beautiful; radiantly attractive (used, apparently, in conjunction with the work of a beautician)
beautiness	beauty; the quality of (almost) beauty
bolsterment	a bolstering strengthening, improvement
congenitive	congenital; inborn; natural

121

♥ contribulate   to cause or add to problems or affliction in others
                                ("contribute" + "tribulate"; see *tribulate*);
                                also "contribulation"

♥ disastrophe   disaster + catastrophe (*gratia* Lou Gottlieb)

dooce   to fire or dismiss in retaliation for online
                                comments, e.g., on blogs, etc.

♥ dystemporaneous   out of sync with the times

♥ fakespert   a phony "expert, with no actual knowledge of the
                                field under discussion (e.g. psychologist "Dr. Phil"
                                explaining viral pandemics)

grammerical   grammatical (incorrectly derived from "grammar")

negatory   no; negative

♥ preimbursement   advance on expenses

profitize   a combination of "profit" and "privatize," spoken
                                by a guest or caller on the Thom Hartmann radio
                                show; possibly an echo term of "monetize"

publicate   publish a secret bit of information (a possible
                                attempt at a back-formation combining
                                "publicize," "publication," and/or "publish")

refudiate   refute + repudiate (*gratia* Sarah Palin)

rigamaroar   loud rigamarole (first heard on television's *Duck
                                Dynasty*)

squirmish   uncomfortable, untenable; another Sarah Palin
                                coinage, a conflation of skirmish (a battle or
                                fight) and "squirm" or "squeamish," apparently
                                describing how Ms. Palin feels about American
                                involvement in the Middle East

♥ substantiable   provable; subject to substantiation by empirical data

♥ tribulate, tribulating   afflict, cause anxiety (a logical back-formation from
                                "tribulation" whose root is the Latin verb
                                "tribulare," meaning "afflict")

♥ truthiness   thank Stephen Colbert for this description of non-
                                fact-based "truth"; an alternate reality that seems
                                true, or could conceivably be true, or is true in
                                part, but not as a whole

♥ unsightful   without insight; lacking the ability to comprehend
                                profound ideas or nuance

                        More neologisms...

Negatives without positives

English speakers use a number of nouns, verbs, adjectives, and idiomatic phrases with negative meanings that don't have positive counterparts in common use. Here are some of my favorites along with the positives I wish existed. (Note that in a few cases the "positive" words exist, but with completely different meanings.) Many of these were first brought to my attention through the late Jack Winter's 1994 comedic essay, "How I Met My Wife."

Disarray	array
Debunk	bunk
Discombobulate	combobulate
Disconcerting	concerting
Disconsolate	consolate
Disgruntled	gruntled
Disheveled	sheveled
Dismayed	mayed
Immaculate	maculate
Incorrigible	corrigible
Indomitable	domitable
Impeccable	peccable
Impetuous	petuous
Impromptu	promptu
Inadvertent	advertent
Incapacitated	capacitated
Inchoate	choate
Incognito	cognito
Incommunicado	communicado
Indefatigable	defatigable
Inept	ept [The archaic meaning of "apt" is "competent" or "capable" but the word is rarely used that way today.]

Inevitable	evitable
Insipid	sipid
Interminable	terminable
Misgivings	givings
Misnomer	nomer
Nonchalant	chalant
Noncommittal	committal
Nondescript	descript
Nonpareil	pareil
Nonplussed	plussed
Persona non grata	persona grata
Unbeknownst	beknownst
Unbridled	bridled
Uncalled-for	called-for
Unflappable	flappable
Ungainly	gainly
Ungodly	godly
Unheard-of	heard-of
Unkempt	kempt
Unmitigated	mitigated
Unnerved	nerved
Unruly	ruly
Unsavory	savory
Unswerving	swerving
Untold	told
Unsung	sung
Untoward	toward
Unwieldy	wieldy

Some Strange Synonyms, Antonyms, & Contranyms

English contains a few word pairs that function as synonyms, antonyms, or both. To "total" something might be adding the full value of a column of numbers—counting everything—or destroying every bit of a car's value—counting it as nothing. "I came to warn you" and "I'm warning you" have quite contrary implications. That's one reason they're called "contranyms" or "contronyms." So be aware: sometimes a word you think you understand just might mean its opposite.

These few pairs form only the beginning of a list; any contributions that add to it will be welcome.

Synonyms despite themselves

best (a foe)	worst (a foe)
dissever (separate into parts)	sever (cut into parts)
flammable	inflammable
ravel	unravel
valuable	invaluable

Schizophrenic words: contranyms

cleave (cling to; stay with)	cleave (cut in two; separate)
depthless (immensely deep)	depthless (shallow, superficial)
dust (spread, as fertilizer or herbicide)	dust (remove, as dirt motes)
hew (cling or adhere to)	hew (chop down; lop off)
oversight (supervision; attention)	oversight (omission; lack of attention)
peruse (examine closely; study)	peruse (skim over quickly)
sanction (allow; permit)	sanction (punish)
total (add all; sum up)	total (destroy utterly, as a car; reduce to nothing)
trim (add decorations)	trim (remove excess)

warn (alert to protect from harm)   warn (threaten with harm)

wear (deteriorate; erode)   wear (resist deterioration; endure)

A Few of My Pet Peeves

Pet peeves seem to appear out of nowhere, but sometimes they're nothing more than irritating reminders of long-ago mistakes committed by or around the peeved person (or "peevee"). I cringe when people incorrectly use "I" in place of "me" because I'm reminded of Mr. Nit's attempts to seem, or become, more sophisticated than he was: the proverbial bright country boy who became "the first in his family to go to college," he never shed his self-consciousness about his roots. Like Mr. Nit, "I"-abusers suffer from the incorrect assumption that the nominative "I" is more sophisticated than the objective "me."

Mrs. Pick, on the other hand, was fluent in five languages, had no self-consciousness about her intellect and vast knowledge, and was blithely willing to correct her children over every grammatical lapse. If we said "Can I go?" instead of "May I go?" Mrs. Pick would call us out; she'd change our "good" to "well" or "le mer" to "la mer" at the drop of a hat, whatever language we might be using at the moment. Worse (for us at least), she taught Russian and German at our school, which meant she also corrected our friends when they stumbled. As a result, some in our crowd gibed us for being under Mrs. Pick's thumb, or, conversely, for being her "teacher's pet"; others resented her pickiness, and still others shamed us by outperforming us in their linguistic prowess.

Many of the peeves peeving me reflect the solecisms my siblings and I committed as children. To this day I can hear Mrs. Pick saying, with some irritation, "You kids know that 'proximity' means 'closeness,' so 'close proximity' is redundant!" Other peeves recall mistakes made by others that embarrassed me on their behalf. For example, on hearing Mr. Nit say, in front of better-spoken friends, "Our kids matter more than anything else to their mother and I," I wanted to hide my head in shame—or (brat that I could be) chastise him with a murmured, "their mother and ME."

I'm also peeved when writers abuse traditional idioms by substituting the wrong word for the idiomatic one. Idioms are one of the factors that give English (or any other language) its color and savor and reflect its history. "Toe the line," for example, is believed to have originated in the British navy, when sailors stood for inspection with their toes—that is, the toes of their boots—aligned along the edge of a plank on deck. The phrase came to mean helping maintain good order, or obeying orders. But we also have a compound word, "towline," used to designate the rope or cable used to tow vehicles or vessels, and many writers mistakenly substitute "tow the line" for "toe the line." And when they do, I pull my hair out. Which just might explain the male pattern baldness that seems to afflict so many language mavens (though not mavennes).

Speaking of tearing my hair out, another thing I'd like to tear out by the roots is the use of "very" with "unique" and other superlatives and absolutes. Something unique is, literally, "one of a kind." It can't be "very one of a kind," and it can't be "very unique." Like "meticulous," "unique" is an absolute adjective (or adverb, with "-ly") that cannot be intensified, and may be only narrowly modified. Occasionally one might say something is "almost unique in the annals of history," or in casual, idiomatic usage, "It's kinda unique, don't ya think?" but for the most part, something *is* unique, or it's not unique.

Similarly, a copy-editor pays meticulous attention to detail, or does not. It's allowable to intensify praise by saying something like, "She is truly meticulous," but if a publisher tells a writer, "He's usually pretty meticulous as a proofreader"—that, to me, would be a signal to bring in another pair of eagle eyes to check for the mistakes he not-so-meticulously overlooked.

So in my view, in general it's better to leave the absolutes absolutely alone.

Many people also have the habit of substituting "I" or "myself" for "me," apparently under the delusion that using "me," even in the objective case, is a sign of illiteracy. It's been drummed into them that "Me and Joey wanted to ..." is wrong, so they change it to "Myself and Joey wanted to ..." as if the longer word must be correct. But "myself" is a reflexive pronoun, not a nominative one; proper usage is "Joey and I wanted to...."

Similarly, people change "She gave it to Joey and me" to "She gave it to Joey and I," believing, like Mr. Nit, that "I" is more refined—and oblivious to the fact that it's ungrammatical and plain wrong. The best way to avoid these solecisms is to kick "Joey" to the curb; if "me" is right by itself ("Give it to me!"), it's right with Joey; if "I" is correct by itself ("I went shopping."), it's right with a companion ("Joey and I went shopping."). And as a reflexive pronoun, "myself" should never be used as the subject of a sentence—except in quotation marks, as here.

Finally, some of my pet peeves reflect word abuses I wish everyone learned at birth, such as the difference between "imply" and "infer."

"Imply" means "to contain or include by necessity" or "to hint or suggest." Thus it refers to the doer or speaker, or, in effect, the subject of the sentence: *Comedy implies humor*, i.e., your statement implies something to me. "Infer" means to draw a conclusion, to "induce or assume." Thus the listener infers—draws *in*—from something heard or understood, or from facts presented. *I infer from your smile that you're happy.*

A good mnemonic (memory aid) uses the "m" and "n" in the two words: "imply" implies "making" a suggestion; "in-fer" suggests "taking in" a conclusion.

If you have pet peeves you'd like to share with me, please do; I'd be glad to add them to the short lists that follow. Again the correct usage is in the column on the left, the incorrect usage on the right.).

Pet Peeve—Incorrect word

Correct usage	Incorrect usage
all right	alright*
bated breath	baited breath (worms taste awful)
bald-faced lie	bold-faced lie
between you and me	between you and I
champing at the bit	chomping at the bit
complementary pairing	complimentary pairing
foment hatred	forment hatred
run the gantlet	run the gauntlet
take for granted	take for granite
could (should, might) have been	could of been
home in on	hone in on
at the lectern (on the podium)	at the podium
notorious (to mean scandalous)	(to mean famous, renowned)
a long row to hoe	a long road to hoe

---

* "Alright" was widely used in 1920s literature, like Agatha Christie's 1922 novels *The Secret Adversary, The Murder of Roger Ackroyd*, and other works. Apparently the word was acceptable in that era, though by the 1960s it was considered incorrect, or at least irregular, in American English.

Pet Peeve—Incorrect word (cont'd)

Correct usage	Incorrect usage
set foot in	step foot in*
supposedly	supposably**
on tenterhooks	on tenderhooks
toe the line	tow the line
tread the boards (present tense)	trod the boards (present tense)
trod the boards (past tense)	
wreak havoc	wreck havoc
wreaked or wrought havoc	wrecked havoc
when worse comes to worst	when worse comes to worse

Pet Peeve—Redundant word or phrase

Correct usage	Incorrect usage
gift	free gift
meticulous	extremely meticulous
nine a.m. or nine in the morning	nine a.m. in the morning
palette	color palette
the point being that... or	the point being, is that...
the point is that ...	
proximity	close proximity
the reason is that ...	the reason why is that ...
strangled	strangled to death
the thing is that	the thing is, is that

Pet Peeve—Redundant word or phrase (cont'd)

Correct usage	Incorrect usage
tuna	tuna fish

---

* "Step foot in" is becoming so widespread, even in major journals, that soon it will be the accepted idiomatic usage, despite cries of despair from traditionalists.

** "Supposably" is the adverb derived from "supposable," meaning "conceivable" or "imaginable" (but not "imagined" or "imaginary"). "Supposedly" means "by repute" or "as claimed," though many people incorrectly use the former to mean the latter.

unique   very unique

Where is she?   Where is she at?

Pet Peeve—Incorrect idiom

Correct usage   Incorrect usage

a couple of minutes (people, etc.)   a couple minutes (people, etc.)

 or a couple more minutes

as far as the [subject] is concerned,   as far as the [subject],

 or ... as for the [subject],

based on   based off of

both of us   the both of us

center on or revolve around   center around

en masse   on [or in] mass

reached fortissimo   reached its crescendo

("crescendo" means a gradual increase, not the final volume)

the proof of the pudding is in the   the proof is in the pudding

 eating

Add your pet peeves here!

And, Finally, Mondegreens

Ah, the mondegreen. As a way to fracture the language, it's a favorite of my friend, fellow editor, copywriter, and super-proofreader Carol Emmet. According to that handy reference site Wikipedia (accessed June 25, 2020):

> A mondegreen is the mishearing or misinterpretation of a phrase as a result of near homophony, in a way that gives it a new meaning. Mondegreens are most commonly created by a person listening to a poem or a lyric in a song; the listener, being unable to clearly hear a lyric, substitutes words that sound similar and make some kind of sense. American writer Sylvia Wright coined the term in 1954, writing that as a girl, when her mother read to her from Percy's *Reliques*, she had misheard the lyric "layd him on the green" in the fourth line of the Scottish ballad "The Bonny Earl of Murray" as "Lady Mondegreen." "Mondegreen" was included in the 2000 edition of the Random House *Webster's College Dictionary*, and in the Oxford English Dictionary in 2002 *Merriam-Webster's Collegiate Dictionary* added the word in 2008.

When I was a child, my mother used to read aloud to me from Percy's *Reliques*, and one of my favorite poems began, as I remember:

> Ye Highlands and ye Lowlands,
> Oh, where hae ye been?
> They hae slain the Earl O' Moray,
> And Lady Mondegreen.

The correct fourth line is "And laid him on the green."

Wright explained the need for a new term: "The point about what I shall hereafter call mondegreens, since no one else has thought up a word for them, is that they are better than the original."

As I go about my daily work as a writer, editor, and publisher, I find that my ears are attuned to listen for, and occasionally hear, mondegreens. Previously I mentioned the ad agency writer who turned "prima donna" into "pre-Madonna"; a similar incident turned "bona fide" into "bonified"! While driving one day I heard a radio ad for a "soup or salad special" at a local restaurant; I went by only to be disappointed that soup wasn't on the menu: they were promoting a "super salad special."

Once at a writers' convention I came in halfway through a conversation that I assumed was about sales success, or lack of same: "... they don't have purchase," someone was saying. Hoping to learn something about turning books (including this one) into established best-sellers, I eavesdropped shamelessly ... until, to my disappointment, I discovered the nice person was talking about a line of pretty, handcrafted birdhouses that were useless because they lacked perches in front of the entry hole. More recently, I caught the end of a video on television in which the Deputy Attorney General of the United States suggested that the administration was pressuring him, saying, "I know what a pile-on feels like." I heard "pylon," and immediately thought of how much more attractive buried power lines are than those that line our highways on tall steel supports.

Though the word is a recent addition to *Webster's*, clearly mondegreens are hardly new. The first one I can remember "discovering," in what is now called middle school (back when it was called junior high) was the fairly common substitution of "youth in Asia" for "euthanasia." Friend Carol recalls mishearing the late Jimi Hendrix's lyric, "Excuse me while I kiss the sky," as "Excuse me while I kiss this guy," and consequently wondering if Hendrix was gay. Another friend recalls that more than 75 years ago, when people sang the well-known lyric, "Gladly the cross I'd bear," his mother was quite confused by her image of a very happy, if cross-eyed, teddy bear. More recently, a friend saw this earnest self-description on a Facebook page: "I took St. Francis of a sissy as my confirmation name."

Writer Jeanne Larsen sent me these wonderful childhood mondegreens: "When I was four or five during WWII, our neighborhood of youngsters held military funerals for every dead bird, mouse, rabbit, etc., that we found. We stood at attention and saluted as my cousin played 'Taps' with a tissue over a comb, and Ozzie the preacher's son ended with the blessing he'd not-quite-learned from his father: 'In the name of the Father, and the Son, and in the hole he goes!' A generation later, listening to 'Lucille' on the car radio as Kenny Rodgers sang about four hungry children and a crop in the field, my young daughter Steph sang along: "with four hundred children and ..."'

The more manuscripts I review, and the more writers I work with on their memoirs, fiction manuscripts, newspaper articles, and websites, the more amazed I am at the ability of creative and analytical minds to weave the several hundred thousand words of modern English into unexpected and sometimes never-before-imagined combinations. Nearly every day I encounter well-educated men and women whose idiosyncratic speech patterns, often learned in childhood, reflect idiomatic usages I'd never heard: "whelp" for "welt" in the South; "liberry" for "library" from upstate New York; "intelligentsia" for "intelligence," invariably misused by Mr. Nit when he wanted to sound more educated than he was (and as a result, sounded less so); and numerous other solecisms and oddities that come to my ears or eyes from time to time.

And the more I realize the breadth, depth, and vitality of the Greco-Latin, Indo-European, Franco-Germanic, Anglo-Saxon, Sanskrit, Urdu, and proto-Slavic language we use each day, the more gladly I remind myself, "What a tasty tongue we have to chew on!"

About the Author

A. D. Reed is a writer and editor who operates the editorial service My Own Editor (www.myowneditor.com) and founded the North Carolina-based publishing imprint Pisgah Press LLC (www.pisgahpress.com).

A lover of languages since childhood, he grew up with a multilingual, Canadian-born Russian émigrée mother who spoke English with a flat Cleveland, Ohio, accent and Russian like a lifelong Muscovite; a father from a south Georgia farm family who spoke carefully and precisely (like many a self-conscious, self-made man) though with a noticeable drawl; an elder sister who became an acclaimed editor in Canada and the Cayman Islands, and an older brother who, after careers as a librarian and teacher (and writing poetry), nits and picks with the best of them.

Their extended family and friends spoke southern, Appalachian, British, Anglo-German, Greek-American, deep country, and transplanted-New-Yorker dialects, among many others—all of which Reed listened to and absorbed with fascination. He studied French, German, Greek, Italian, Latin, and Russian as a high school and college student, becoming fluent in some languages, competent in others; but his first love remains the elegant, flexible, surprising, often incomprehensible, sometimes ridiculous, always delightful mélange of tongues that has gradually evolved into the modern American English language.

Also available from Pisgah Press

Letting Go: Collected Poems 1983-2003   Donna Lisle Burton
$14.95
Way Past Time for Reflecting
$17.95
From Roots ... to Wings
$17.95

Gabriel's Songbook   Michael A. Cody
$17.95   FINALIST, FEATHERED QUILL AWARDS, FICTION
A Twilight Reel: Stories
$17.95   GOLD MEDAL WINNER, FEATHERED QUILL AWARDS, SHORT STORIES

Musical Morphine: Transforming Pain One Note at a Time   Robin Russell Gaiser
$17.95   FINALIST, USA BOOK AWARDS FOR HEALTH: ALTERNATIVE MEDICINE
Open for Lunch
$17.95

Shade   H. N. Hirsch
$22.95
Fault Line
$22.95

I Like It Here! Adventures in the Wild & Wonderful World of Theatre   C. Robert Jones
$30.00
                        LANKY TALES FOR TWEENS
Lanky Tales, Vol. I: The Bird Man & other stories
$9.00
Lanky Tales, Vol. II: Billy Red Wing & other stories
$9.00
Lanky Tales, Vol. III: A Good and Faithful Friend & other stories
$9.00
The Mystery at Claggett Cove
$9.00

The Last of the Swindlers   Peter Loewer
$17.95

Swords in their Hands: George Washington and the Newburgh Conspiracy   Dave Richards
$24.95   FINALIST, USA BOOK AWARDS FOR HISTORY

Trang Sen: A Novel of Vietnam   Sarah-Ann Smith
$19.50

Invasive Procedures: Earthquakes, Calamities, & poems from the midst of life   Nan Socolow
$17.95

Deadly Dancing   THE RICK RYDER MYSTERY SERIES   RF Wilson
$15.95
Killer Weed
$14.95
The Pot Professor
$15.95

To order:

Pisgah Press, LLC
PO Box 9663, Asheville, NC 28815-0663
www.pisgahpress.com

as the bumper sticker says ...
visualize whirled peas.

To order by mail or online, please contact:

Pisgah Press
PO Box 9663   Asheville, NC 28815-0663
www.pisgahpress.com
pisgahpress@gmail.com
828-301-8968